THE CONFIDENT WOMAN

Other Books by Ingrid Trobisch

The Joy of Being a Woman
On Our Way Rejoicing
Learning to Walk Alone
Hidden Strength
An Experience of Love, *with Elisabeth Rötzer*

Books by Walter Trobisch

All a Man Can Be
I Loved a Girl
I Married You
Love Is a Feeling to Be Learned
Longing for Love
Love Yourself
My Beautiful Feeling, *with Ingrid Trobisch*
My Journey Homeward

The Confident Woman

❀   *Finding Quiet Strength in*   ❀
a Turbulent World

❀

INGRID TROBISCH

HarperSanFrancisco
A Division of HarperCollins*Publishers*

Quotations from the Bible are from the Revised Standard Version and the New International Version unless otherwise stated.

THE CONFIDENT WOMAN: *Finding Quiet Strength in a Turbulent World.* Copyright © 1993 by Ingrid Trobisch. All rights reserved. Printed in the United States of America. No part of this book may be used or reproduced in any manner whatsoever without written permission except in the case of brief quotations embodied in critical articles and reviews. For information address HarperCollins Publishers, 10 East 53rd Street, New York, NY 10022.

First Edition
Library of Congress Cataloging-in-Publication Data
Trobisch, Ingrid Hult.
    The confident woman: finding quiet strength in a turbulent
    world / Ingrid Trobisch.—1st ed.
          p.   cm.
    Includes bibliographical references.
    ISBN 0–06–068552-2 (alk. paper)
    1. Women—Religious life. 2. Woman (Christian theology).
    3. Confidence—Religious aspects—Christianity.   I. Title.
    BV4527.T76   1993
    248.8'43—dc20   92–56741
                                              CIP

93 94 95 96 97 ❖ HAD 10 9 8 7 6 5 4 3 2 1
This edition is printed on acid-free paper that meets the American National Standards Institute Z39.48 Standard.

*For my mothers, sisters, daughters
—and the men who love them.*

Contents

ACKNOWLEDGMENTS

Special thanks to Clayton Carlson, Roland Seboldt, and Ronald Klug, master editors, who provided the structure and strategy of organization for this book.

—To my daughter Katrine Stewart whose words you will find on these pages interspersed with mine;
—to my daughter Ruth Weissensteiner, who encouraged and cheered me on;
—to my three sons, Daniel, David, and Stephen, who kept the computer going, typed when my wrists were broken, and gave me wise feedback;
—to my niece Ann and granddaughter Virginia who helped in special ways;
—and to my friends and coworkers who surrounded me with prayer and love during gestation and birth of this book, my deep gratefulness.

Ingrid Trobisch

The Crisis in Confidence

"How can you be confident in this crazy, mixed-up world?" my friends ask. "Everything is changing. We want to be valued and validated, but where do we find our mentors and models?"

One woman said to me, "I believe that my grandmother was a confident woman, but my mother wasn't. The values my grandmother had were no longer valid for her. And I'm often just as confused, because I don't know where to find a role model."

This morning I received a mail-order catalog with the latest women's fashions. "A confident you" was written in script across the pages. I was ready to toss another piece of mail in the wastebasket when I saw these words on the envelope: "Stuck, stalled, snowbound, or stranded? No problem. You've got the Confidence Card." That's just what I need, I thought. *If I only had it, all my problems would be solved.*

Another friend, whose husband is a pastor, said, "My husband is helpless when he has to deal with 'whipped women' in his professional and personal life. He tries to counsel them as any good pastor would, but he says their hearts are like sieves. Any good thing he says or does for them goes right through. How can we help them?"

Feeling confused and defeated, these 'whipped women'—that is, women who feel as though the world had raced off and left them choking in the dust—are presented with the challenge of new roles and expectations. The traditional roles of wife and mother, important as they are, often do not extend over a lifetime. There are women who have not yet married or who are no longer married. Moreover, today women can choose from a wider job market. When I was a young girl, by contrast, I wanted to be a teacher; my sister Veda wanted to be a nurse; and my sister Eunie, a mother. That was about it. New opportunities for women mean that they often need to retrain and start anew.

These changes cause more moving around, with a loss of community and traditional support groups. This absence of stable community weakens a woman's confidence. I remember those terrible feelings of aloneness when I moved from my home of eighteen years and my comfortable circle of friends to a new community. It was hard to go to church alone and wonder if anybody would talk to me, besides the handshake and greeting of the pastor at the door. No one there knew about my husband, who had died three years earlier, or my children, who were all young adults and doing their own thing. My family had been a great part of my identity, but now I had to reach out to others or be filled with self-pity.

I am not alone in facing these hindrances. Other women tell me of their struggles not to wallow in self-pity or to be considered second-class citizens. "I want to believe in myself," "I want to be a woman of quiet confidence," they tell me. "Where do I begin?"

In her book *The Wounded Woman*, Linda Leonard describes her own journey to wholeness and confidence. She says women "feel alienated from their center because they are cut off from important parts of themselves. It is as though they have a mansion for their home, but are only living in a few of the rooms."[1]

Leonard cites Mirabai, an Indian poet, who was exuberant after finding her own feminine center and the full strength of her womanhood. Mirabai says, "In her confidence, a woman's self-pity leaves." Instead of a wounded woman, the result of this confidence is a beautiful woman whose ego is not fragile like fine porcelain but can stand up under pressure like tempered Swedish steel.

One of my own role models is Reinhild. I met her at our wedding in Mannheim, Germany, in 1952, and over the years we have become deep friends. I once asked her, "Reinhild, how do you learn how to love?" "By letting yourself be loved" was her prompt answer.

Her eighty-five-year-old mother was present and said to me, "Reinhild is the happiest woman I know—but why? She lost everything during the war—her father, her husband, even her home."

But Reinhild had found faith. I saw this woman radiating confidence and God's great peace and love wherever she went. She was the principal of a large school in Mannheim. Before the first week of school had passed, she knew by heart the names of all the children in her school. "They are my family," she said.

She was a successful administrator. She told me one of her secrets: "I always finish what's on my desk before I go to bed." Whenever I met any of her former pupils, their faces would light up when I mentioned her name. Her presence had changed the whole city because of the lives she had influenced.

Since her retirement, Reinhild has left her well-ordered home every winter from November to May to go to Israel at her own expense. She works long hours there at one of the hospices for German-speaking Jews, helping them to die in dignity and peace.

Another confident woman is Sharon, a nurse and administrator at a large hospital in the Chicago area. One of her coworkers described her to me:

Sharon is courteous, bold, and gently outspoken when action or correction is needed. She is a good listener, tactful and concerned, sincerely caring about people (but not so deeply as to become burned out), honest yet very practical. A shrewd businesswoman, Sharon has a quick mind, good judgment (when to give an appropriate action or word), is wise, and knows suffering. (She has lost many children; only one remains.) Her original ambition was to have "lots and lots" of children. Now she has more than a thousand full-time employees under her charge. She is very devoted yet not a workaholic, trustworthy, clear-minded, determined (sometimes stubborn), and dependable. She is also dignified, well-dressed yet genuinely respectful and humble. She has the ability to "let go and let God" when it's apparent that "it wasn't meant to be."

The portrait of the confident woman in Proverbs 31 is certainly a role model for us.

> Her husband has full confidence in her and lacks
>   nothing of value. . . .
> She considers a field and buys it; out of her earn-
>   ings she plants a vineyard.
> She sets about her work vigorously; her arms are
>   strong for her tasks.
> She sees that her trading is profitable, and her
>   lamp does not go out at night. . . .
> She is clothed with strength and dignity; she can
>   laugh at the days to come.
> She speaks with wisdom, and faithful instruction is
>   on her tongue. . . .
> Give her the reward that she has earned, and let
>   her works bring her praise at the city gate.
>   (Prov. 31:11, 16–18, 25, 26, 31, NIV)

How is it possible to become a woman of quiet confidence in our fast-changing society, where all values seem to be questioned, where traditional roles are challenged, where the ground seems to shift beneath our feet?

As I reflect on my own life and the lives of many women I have known through the years, I am convinced that confidence can be learned and developed. In the pages that follow we will look at the process whereby we can grow in quiet confidence.

In part 1 we will explore how we can be confident in our identity, knowing and accepting ourselves, including those painful questions about gender and what it means to be a whole woman, discovering our roots and our place in the world, recognizing our gifts, and developing new skills.

In part 2 we will look at how you can be confident in relationships—with other women, as a single, with men, and with the children in our lives.

Part 3 explores the way confidence grows out of inner strength as we learn to look for meaning in suffering, seek God's guidance, set goals, make the most of our time, and find ways each day to deepen our friendship with God.

My prayer for each of you is that as you read these pages and reflect on your own life, the Spirit of God will develop in you that quietness and confidence that he has promised will be your strength (Isaiah 30:15).

I

Confident in Your Identity

❀

❀ 1 ❀

Knowing Who You Are

Knowing who we are is the first step to confidence. A confident woman does not run around looking for herself, because she has learned to accept who she is physically, emotionally, and mentally. "It's the job of every woman to forget herself, but how can she do that if she doesn't know who she is?" said Simone de Beauvoir, a great French woman author. The struggle to know ourselves is unending. It's a lifelong journey, so why not get started.

Confidence begins in your heart. It's the feeling of being special, of knowing that you are unique. Just as there are no two snowflakes exactly the same, so God has created each one of us as an individual. We can be confident in our uniqueness. Our presence and presentation are generated by our confidence in the way we look, and we can even have the courage to be different. To become the one I am created to be, isn't that my great work in life?

Our presence, the sort of persons we are, can define us more than the tasks and activities that fill our days. We are called to be not human "doings" but human "beings." Don't we often feel so busy doing that there is nothing left inside? If we are in danger of giving ourselves away before we even know who we are, how can we be confident women? First we learn to be in order to do, rather than to do in order to be. It may take us a lifetime, but it's worth the struggle.

Eleanor Roosevelt shared the wisdom of her life experience in her book *You Learn by Living*. She said that self-knowledge is the first step to confidence and maturity. "You have to be honest with yourself. You must try to understand truthfully what makes you do things or feel things. Until you have been able to face the truth about yourself you cannot be really sympathetic or understanding in regard to what happens to other people. But it takes courage to face yourself and acknowledge what motivates you in the things you do."[1]

Know What You Can Do Well

Often we do not know our own gifts. That's why it's a great help to self-knowledge if we have family and friends who can tell us honestly, "This is what you do well."

I remember the first time Ezra, an African pastor, told me that my gift was to explain to men what a woman is. His words, affirming a gift I did not even know I had, set the stage for that decade of my life. I wrote five little booklets for African husbands, entitled *Understanding Your Wife*. It took a year for me to write each booklet, describing the different facets of a woman's reproductive life, how her body works, and how she feels. My children were still quite young, and writing was hard and lonely work for me. But I took just one step at a time.

Soon these booklets were circulating all over Africa in their French and English editions. A German editor saw them and said, "We need these in German." And from there they came to the United States, where they were published in one volume, entitled *The Joy of Being a Woman and What a Man Can Do*.[2]

I share this experience because it all started when I listened to Ezra tell me, "This is your gift." When someone helps you recognize your gifts, listen, because it's an important part of self-knowledge. Learn to value your abilities, whether they are organizing shelves and drawers, writing a legal brief, baking bread, making children feel loved, doing medical research, arranging flowers, or driving a school bus.

In writing this book I keep my five daughters in mind (that includes my daughters-in-love). I see with great clarity their individual gifts. One is a mystic and has a bridal relationship to her Lord. Another is a musician and shows me what true beauty is. Another is a mother in a classroom of very troubled children, where she brings light into their darkness; she also feeds them breakfast, knowing that most of them have left home without it. Another has the gift of writing clear, to-the-point sentences and paragraphs. Another daughter has great intuition, which she combines with practical medical knowledge; she is an encourager. I also think of my sisters and my nieces, those wonderful "can-do" women. And then I think of my "adopted" sisters, daughters, mothers—those valiant women throughout the world who live in hard places and whom I respect and admire.

Understanding Your Family of Origin

If we want to know who we are, we have to know where we came from. In John Steinbeck's *Grapes of Wrath,* Ma says to Pa as their family prepares to leave the Dust Bowl in Oklahoma, "But, Pa, how will our children know who they are, if they don't know where they came from?"

It helps to know not only where we grew up but also where our ancestors came from. What kind of country made them who they were? Do we have family traditions from that region or country?

We also need to look at our birth order. A first-born or only child is going to face life differently than a second-born or even a third-born. Each position has advantages and disadvantages. The birth order of a husband and a wife will also have a lot to do with their being comfortable together. If a first-born daughter marries a first-born son, there may be a real struggle for understanding and for power.

I had two older brothers, so I was in third place in our family, yet I was the eldest daughter. I used to think that was a disadvantage until I talked it over with my mentor, Theo Bovet, one of

Europe's pioneer marriage counselors. "No," he said, "the eldest daughter in a family knows how to carry responsibility. Because you have five brothers, two of them older, you feel comfortable with men and can work with them." He helped me to know and understand my birth order. My husband was the eldest of three children. He had a sister my age with whom he was very comfortable. Because of the good relationship with his sister (and his mother), he was not threatened by women, and I as his wife reaped the benefits.

What is your ethnic background? Adeline, a close friend who lived with me for three years, was of Native American background. She had a special gift for understanding plants. They all seemed to respond when she talked to them and placed them at just the right spot in the sun or shade. One day she told me of her great-great-grandmother who had come to the Ozarks when the Cherokees were forced to leave their well-cultivated gardens and settlements in the south. They were all to live on reservations designated for them in Oklahoma. Many died on the march, the infamous Trail of Tears. Some left the trail and settled in the Ozarks. I visited the grave of Adeline's ancestors, just outside Springfield, and wept with her as she told me of their suffering.

One day I stood at the grave of my own great-grandmother near Kearney, Nebraska. She had come across the Atlantic on a small Swedish sailing vessel with four small children. Her husband, Svante Lind, who had gone ahead, had sent her the boat fare twice because a swindler intercepted it the first time. (In 1873 the cost of ship passage for one adult from Sweden to New York was fifty-five dollars.) My grandmother was eight years old during this sea voyage. Her parents had made a courageous decision to leave a settled, though limited, existence to come to the vast prairies of Nebraska as homesteaders. When I visited Sweden, I found my grandmother's birthplace, stood at the font where she was baptized, and found a part of my identity in that location.

My friend Adeline did the same when she stood at her great-great-grandmother's grave. We talked about the confident women that our grandmothers had been, each in her own way. "But now it's different," Adeline said. "In your book please tell women how they can be validated, how they can rise out of passivity to tell others their own needs."

Recognizing the Stages of Life

Another important help to self-knowledge is to understand that we live life by stages or chapters. We can think of our years as being divided into seven-year cycles, each cycle representing a new stage of life. It takes seven years for a newborn to grow through infancy and become a schoolchild. After seven more years the child becomes an adolescent. At the age of twenty-one, one is a young adult; at the age of twenty-eight, a more mature adult.

In her book *Passages* Gail Sheehy writes about the mysteries of the life cycle. A part of the "pulling-up roots" stage of the late teens and early twenties is the de-idealizing of the parents (or parent substitute) so that one can learn to have confidence in one's own judgment. Sheehy says that before the 1960s, "it was barely conceivable that a girl child could embark on Being Somebody before her father had escorted her to the altar under a fingertip illusion veil. The door to adulthood would be magically unlocked by wedlock. . . . This form still persists as the most favored route to female identity: the 'complete me' marriage."[3]

These women believe that a man will complete them and keep them safe. "Marriage is a half step, a way to leave home without losing home. . . . What such a marriage brings instead is a foreclosure of identity. The commitment to being a wife is made before the individual is allowed, or allows herself, to struggle with and select from the possible life choices."[4]

The problem was that most young women wouldn't dare or weren't allowed to have an identity crisis. The result was that they never grew up.

Nora, the main character in Henrik Ibsen's play *The Dollhouse,* is a woman caught in this struggle. "I was the doll-child of my father," she says to her husband, "and since then I have lived in the doll-house of my husband, but now your doll is taken away."

Although they had been married eight years and had three children, Nora and her husband had never talked seriously. He calls her his "song-bird," his "little squirrel," and she plays along with him. "If we were to talk," she tells him, "then we would both have to change so much that our life together would become a marriage."[5]

The Dollhouse, written in 1879, has been called the greatest play of the nineteenth century, yet, like all classics, it has a message for us today. It mirrors the inner battles of many women, both young and old, who were never allowed to quite grow up and become confident individuals.

Grace Kimathi, a confident woman, a wife and the mother of four, lives in Nairobi, Kenya. She is one of the co-workers in the family life ministry my husband, Walter, and I founded in 1965. Grace helped us to answer hundreds of letters that African young people wrote after reading our books. "What do you tell them," I once asked her, "when they ask for advice on choosing their future partners?" "I always tell them to take their time, because marriage does not bring fulfillment to unfulfilled people." There's only one thing harder than living alone, and that is to live with another person. Yet only the one who is capable of living alone is able to live with another person and make a success of marriage.

All of life is a struggle for maturity, with its predictable crises of adulthood. We cannot afford to jump over any of its stages. They are all good: The pulling-up roots stage; the trying twenties, when we try to take hold in the adult world; the catch-30, when most of us begin putting down roots and sending out new shoots; the deadline decade of the midthirties, when we know we've reached the halfway mark and time starts to squeeze us. By the midforties, we have hopefully gained a new stability. Depending on how we face our midlife crisis, we will either become resigned or renewed.[6]

For a woman, part of the midlife crisis is learning to understand what's happening in her body. A confident woman will learn to love her body when it is no longer young. She knows that menopause is not the end but a new beginning. When it's completed, she is no longer under the hormonal changes of her cycle. She is able to depend on herself. As a school principal, my friend Reinhild told me that the decade between fifty and sixty were the best years of her life. She didn't miss a day of school, while her younger colleagues often had to have sick leave. It was her experience that after menopause, women, if they were healthy, could depend on their bodies more.

In their book *Menopause and Mid-Life,* Robert and Mary Wells, who direct a menopause center in California, write:

> Women who handle menopause best are those who have good self-esteem, who have a track record of dealing well with stress, and who have many friends, lots of outside interests and activities, and good marriages with supportive husbands. These women tend to be less affected by the menopausal changes that are taking place in their bodies.
>
> Also, women whose mothers managed their own menopause with relative ease tend to follow suit, suggesting some hereditary influences at work. This may be explained as well by similar temperaments or the cultural similarities they share.[7]

Dr. Bovet, our own marriage counselor, called menopause "femininity lost and then refound in a more wonderful way."

In Africa a woman is considered a bearer of wisdom when she has completed menopause. She is respected and listened to when she gives her advice. Many great chiefs, in fact, have one or more older women close to their throne rooms, so they are available for consultation in a time when great wisdom is needed.

One seventy-year-old person said, "I am very surprised to find out how much I enjoy aging—that process by which you bring together and integrate all the stages of life. I find that I have more to do now that is fun. I don't have to be so concerned about everything. You get a kind of intelligence that I would call wisdom in the last stage of life. This is why the Indians called on their oldest braves to give them advice."

"Please write something about getting old, before you are old," my editor in Germany said recently. Here are some of the things I'm learning as I grow older:

A Heightened Sense of Time

Although older people are free to spend their time the way they want, they also have less of it. Time does not last forever, and therefore I do not want to waste a single moment of it. If I make good use of it, I will actually have more of it. Eleanor Roosevelt put it right when she said, "If I have something to do, I just do it."

I've found that there's nothing more fatiguing than the eternal hanging-on of an uncompleted task. I have three of them staring me in the face right now. From years of trying to do a tightrope act of balancing different tasks, I have learned to be realistic. Not one of these projects will be finished quickly, but I can make a plan for the day that allows me to spend some time on each project. "Do a little every day," my mother-in-law used to tell me when I looked at the pile of unanswered mail on my desk, the overflowing mending basket, and the unstraightened drawers. Every little success experience keeps me motivated and gives me the momentum to keep going. My reward—a walk in the crisp air of the Ozarks before dark.

Maturity Through Suffering

Theo Bovet used to say, "There are only two kinds of people: those who become old, and those who become mature." God's goal for us is always maturity. When we suffer courageously, we come out stronger, and we lose our fear of the future. We have faced that which is most difficult, and we are still alive. A German proverb says, "That which doesn't kill me makes me tougher."

"God whispers to us in our pleasures . . . but shouts in our pains," C. S. Lewis reminds us.[8] Sometimes God has to touch the tender spot in our lives, and out of the touching comes a great new healing that enables us to be who we were intended to be.

The Joy of Grandparenting

"Grandparenting is the only stage of life that there's nothing wrong with," a friend told me. That was before I had grandchildren. I can only agree with her now that I have eleven of my own. There's a new zest for living with a new generation, and a greater sense of connection with the cycle of life. The joy of children without the pain is very satisfying.

Foster grandparenting brings great satisfaction to those who have no grandchildren of their own. Many children never get to know their real grandparents because of early death or geographical separation (as was the case for our children), yet they know the joy of having a foster grandfather or grandmother to fill that void.

Knowing Your Personality and Emotional Responses

One of the most helpful experiences of my adult life was to learn to know my own temperament and emotional reactions. In our Quiet Waters retreats now held throughout the world, my co-workers and I offer to each individual the opportunity of taking the Taylor-Johnson Temperament Analysis. This can be especially helpful to couples, for the husband and wife first describe themselves individually and then each other. We then have a clear profile for each partner: their strengths and the areas where they need to work. In a private talk we give them suggestions for making their relationship more effective. It is not a judgment but simply an inventory of what they have to work with in their emotional and temperamental makeup. Understanding each other in this way is often a revealing and helpful experience.

Another tool for personality insight is the Myers-Briggs Type Indicator. Carl Jung, the Swiss psychiatrist, said each person is born with a personality predisposition that affects the way a person approaches life. The Myers-Briggs inventory suggests that each predisposition expresses itself in a different life-style or orientation to the outer world.

Christ accepts us just where we are, but he does not leave us there. He wants us to work in those areas where we may be hurting ourselves or our loved ones.

Knowing Your Limitations and Your Dangers

We can learn the most from our own mistakes. In fact the only real mistakes we make are those from which we don't learn. Experience is the best teacher, but often we need loving friends to help us set the limits.

How thankful my husband and I were for a steering committee with whom we met regularly when we were organizing our new ministry, which we called *Family Life Mission*. We would share with our committee invitations that had come to us, the projects that we were working on, and our financial concerns. They were clear in telling us to be realistic: "You can't do this trip to Finland this year. Let's put it on next year's calendar." "You forgot to write in your vacation time on your schedule." "You have too many retreats planned for the fall."

Since I have been learning to live alone after Walter's death, one of the hardest things is to know my limits and danger points. I need kind friends and co-workers—and my children—to tell me this. Just as we have a blind spot in driving a car so our gifts can also become blind spots and dangers if we don't have someone to warn us.

Try putting that little word *too* in front of your gifts and see what happens:

- Generous is good, but too generous can become careless.
- Economical is good, but too economical can become stingy.
- Orderly is good, but too orderly can mean rigid, with a loss of spontaneity.
- Active is good, but too much activity can become a flight from simply being.

When I take a photograph, I must first decide all the things I don't want in my picture. The same is true in painting and sketching. The first decision you have to make is your frame of reference. That may mean eliminating even some of the beautiful things.

Think not only of your gifts but also of your dangers and the boundaries that God in his wisdom has set up in your life. Acknowledging and accepting our limitations are the keys to finding out who we really are rather than who we think we ought to be.

But it is not enough to know ourselves. We also want to be ready to take the next step: to accept who we are, warts and all.

❋ 2 ❋

Learning to Accept Yourself

"True happiness comes when you can look at yourself and like what you see." These words on a poster express the goal of this chapter.

It's not enough just to know ourselves. We also want to say yes to who we are, and sometimes that takes courage. If we can't accept ourselves, we can't love ourselves. If we can't love ourselves, we won't be able to love others.

"I was a mistake." "I never liked myself." Have you heard such words, or said them yourself? When speaking at one of our seminars, my late husband, Walter, would quietly say, "No one is born with the ability to love herself or himself. Self-love or self-esteem is either acquired or it is nonexistent. The one who does not acquire it or who acquires it insufficiently either is not able to love others at all or loves them only insufficiently."

Because this ability to accept oneself is often undeveloped especially in Christian circles, he would say, "a type of Christian develops who loves out of duty and who in this way tortures not only others but also himself or herself."

When we reject ourselves, we project our attitude of ourselves onto others. I was trying to get this point across as I gave a lecture to a group of passengers on board the SS *Norway,* a large cruise ship. The ship's comedian was present and had to leave in the middle of the lecture. As he made for the door, he said in an inimitable voice, first pointing to himself and then to the passengers: "Listen to her. If I can't love me, then I can't love you." I learned later that he was a recovering alcoholic and that this truth had been one of the stepping-stones to a new life for him.

"Well and good," you say, "but where do I begin? If I try to do it myself, it's like pulling myself out of a swamp by my own bootstraps. The harder I try, the deeper I sink. And I don't have anyone around me who will help me. I've been put down all my life."

Accepting God's Acceptance

There is only one way that I know to break this vicious cycle, and that is to accept help from outside. The words of Paul in Rom. 15:7 are helpful: "Accept one another, therefore, as Christ has accepted us for the glory of God" (NEB).

We are already accepted, these words mean, because through Christ, God took the first step. "We love, because he first loved us" (1 John 4:19). "Nothing you could do could make God love you more than he does right now," said Pastor Lloyd Ogilvie at Hollywood Presbyterian Church.

It took me a long time to learn this, because it was too simple. I thought that faith was something that I had to work up myself, instead of being a gift placed in my empty, outstretched hands. Faith is like coming home, running right straight into the arms of my heavenly Father, just as I could do with my earthly father. When he came home from work, I would run through the orchard path to be the first to meet him. Then he would put down his lunch pail, open his arms, and embrace me.

Steadfast love are two words used throughout the Old Testament. No matter how impossible and stubborn God's people were, he still loved them with unlimited, unconditional love. In the words Nehemiah prayed, "You are a God ready to forgive, gracious and merciful, slow to anger and abounding in steadfast love" (Neh. 9:17).

It is true that Christ accepts us as we are: "Him who comes to me I will not cast out" (John 6:37). But this is just the beginning.

God's acceptance of us is the base where we begin work. Luther stated in the fourth thesis that he nailed on the church door in Wittenberg, "God's love does not love that which is worthy of being loved, but it creates that which is worthy of being loved."[1] This is a lifelong process, and it does not happen without "growing pains."

Our mentor, Theo Bovet, put it this way in one of his books: "If I love myself in the right way, then it is impossible for me to remain standing still. On the contrary, I want to change so that I can become that which God desires me to become. In the same way we should also love our neighbor."[2]

Learning to Accept Your Physical Self

I remember visiting my mother when she was almost eighty years old. She was the hostess for her neighborhood club, and after a sumptuous buffet lunch of special dishes each woman prepared, my mother invited the guests to join in a time of devotion. "But first," she said, "I want you all to be quiet for a moment and think of one thing that you like about yourself—preferably about your physical body." The women, all in their sixties and seventies, protested, "Why didn't you ask us what we don't like about our bodies? That would be easier."

Finally one of them said, "I like my smile." Another, "My hair is naturally curly, so I never need to get a permanent." Another said, "I can eat as much as I want and I never gain weight." I waited eagerly to hear what Mother would say. "I like my good strong body," she said. "It has served me well." This was a good exercise in self-acceptance. Try it out with your friends, and you'll see it's not easy.

What about our wrinkles as we grow older? Some women who can afford it try to combat them with frequent face-lifts, collagen treatments, or with shots that cause relaxed muscles under the skin to firm up. The only trouble with the latter procedure is that it has to be repeated twice a year at around two thousand dollars a treatment. Dr. Bovet called the wrinkles he tenderly observed on his wife's face (she was ten years older than he) "the shorthand of her life." Mark Twain once said, "Wrinkles should merely indicate where the smiles have been." For men who have trouble accepting their wife's wrinkles, I would like to ask, "Is your love only skin-deep?"

Women everywhere seem to want to connect their sense of self-worth with their current body weight. Dr. Art Ulene, medical adviser for NBC, said on the "Today Show," "If only I could get women to separate their sense of self-worth from their body weight."

He knew what cosmetic surgeons know, that some women are never satisfied. Even if they reach their ideal weight, if they didn't like their bodies before, they won't like them even after they lose weight. Often when a woman has an operation to improve the shape of her nose, she will not be satisfied with that operation alone and may even become addicted to cosmetic surgery. I liked what Barbra Streisand said recently: "Now at the age of fifty, I have finally grown into my face and can accept it."

An attractive woman in her forties came to meet me at the airport. I told her how beautiful she was. She said that she had worked for a year to take off ten extra pounds, but that she was very disappointed.

"Why?" I asked.

"Because I thought it would make my marriage better," she said, "but it hasn't. We still have the same struggles."

Perhaps her real struggle was just to accept herself as she was and then to accept her husband as he was. Psychologist Susan Wooley says, "Women throughout history have been led to believe if they look better, it'll fix everything. . . . Diets don't keep the weight off. People who lose weight and regain it take an emotional battering. Dieters blame themselves when the programs aren't working.

"The trend now is away from restrictive dieting. Instead, eat prudently, cut fat and exercise moderately—walk four or five times a week. Then the weight you end up with is what you should weigh." She adds, "Make peace with who you are—which includes the body you drew in that genetic lottery at birth."[3]

To love being a woman means having a thankful attitude for what we have been given. This is what my elderly mother was trying to get across to her peer group. It reminds me of what Golda Meir, for many years prime minister of Israel, said when speaking to schoolchildren in Milwaukee: "If you don't believe in yourself, who's going to? But if you believe only in yourself, of what use are you?"

Meir went on to say, "I was never a beauty, and when I was old enough to understand the importance of it, I was sorry. When I looked in the mirror I realized it was something I was never going to have. But then, I found out what I wanted to do in life, and being pretty lost its importance. I was forced in this way to develop my inner resources."[4]

Golda Meir was indeed one of the great women of our times. When I read her autobiography, I was impressed above all by the help she gave to the less developed countries in Africa. David Ben-Gurion, one of the founding fathers of present Israel, said teasingly of her, "She's the best man we have."

Balancing the Masculine and Feminine Within

God can speak truth from many sources. Throughout four decades of ministry in Africa, Europe, and the United States, three of them together with my husband, Walter, I searched diligently for practical answers to human problems. Although we may disagree with much of what Carl Jung has said, his portrayal of the masculine and feminine within each one of us ("animus" and "anima") can shed light on Gen. 1:27b, "male and female he created them." The word *animus* refers to the male pole of our being, *anima* to the female. None of us is solely male or female. We are bipolar, both male and female. We are not bisexual, but we express ourselves in one or the other pole of our being.

In their book *Restoring the Christian Family,* counselors John and Paula Sanford give this explanation of the anima and animus.

> Both poles operate in us whether we are a man or a woman. In the anima reside feeling, nurture, care, intuition, sensitivity, receiving, spontaneity, and desire. Love participates both in the animus and the anima, but because of its association with emotion, we list it as part of the anima. Art as a skill manifests in the logic and structure of the animus. But the intuitive sense of art originates in the highest imaginative and sensitive faculties of the anima. . . .
>
> The other side of us is the animus. In it are logic, structure, authority, principle, idea, aggression, thrust or drive, and creativity. One sees immediately that these divisions are just too neat; you can't split people like that. We are too complex. And women's rightists might object strenuously to these arbitrary delineations (stereotypes) of what is male or female, which actually may come more from cultural definitions than from what God created us to be. But sometimes an oversimplification gives us a springboard for understanding, so let's use it and hold our reservations as a *counterbalance* in the back of our minds.

The Sanfords go on to say, "Until we allow the Lord Jesus Christ to fill that God-shaped space in us, we will demand our mate to fill it. The Lord is the only whole one, who can complete both sides of our being. . . . If we do not find our balance in him, we will not achieve it in our relationship with our mate."[5]

In one illuminating statement, C. S. Lewis said that "spiritually there should be a little man inside of every woman and a little woman inside of every man."[6]

I have found this statement a helpful point of reference when teaching both singles and couples about the necessity of balance in saying yes to both masculinity and femininity within. It is precisely in achieving this balance that we become whole persons, confident men and women.

Why is it so difficult for women to get in touch with the "little man" inside? I asked my son Daniel, who as a Christian psychologist and counselor has spent many years studying and teaching about the crisis in femininity, "How does a girl become a confident woman? How does she get in touch not only with her femininity but also with her masculinity, so that she can become a whole person?" Daniel's answer was simple: "She must be recognized by her father."

Often this does not happen, and so she goes into marriage without being ready for it. She then looks for affirmation from her young husband, who more than likely is unable to cope with this need. He may have been unaffirmed himself in his masculinity. He cannot give what he does not have. That is when both sexes make the mistake of fleeing into eroticism, thinking, Better two warm bodies than a cold, lonely heart. They look for romantic love to satisfy their deepest needs. According to psychologist Robert Johnson, we can only expect this kind of love to last anywhere from three months to three years. "What we need," he says, "is the stirring-the-oatmeal kind of love."[7]

As a word of explanation, we are not talking here about sexism, that mental picture we often have of what a woman or man should be like, but of something far beyond that. We're talking not about a woman becoming a man but how she can become more of a woman. Neither are we talking about unisex. Rather we are talking about becoming more whole and that can only happen when our wounds are healed.

How can this happen if there has been no father to recognize and call forth the little man in his daughter? Leanne Payne, author and leader of Pastoral Care Ministry retreats throughout the world, tells of her experience of growing up without a father.

Though my mother and my aunt were affirming, free, whole women who affirmed me in so very many ways, they could not affirm me as a woman and therefore as a person. They could not bring me out of puberty and into self-acceptance the way an affirming father or father-figure could have done. I was past thirty when I began working through the failure to accept myself. I learned to come to God the Father for affirmation. He then not only affirmed me as a woman and as a full person in my own right, but ministered into my life the masculine giftedness I lacked because of being fatherless. He gave me the power that enabled me to better contain the feminine world of meaning—to orient it, direct it, order it, and then to take full responsibility for it.[8]

Feminine Energy

What is feminine energy? Linda Leonard, in her book *On the Way to the Wedding,* speaks of the feminine "spirit" and the masculine "heart" that have to be developed in each individual. If this does not happen, we will have only the "wounded woman," Leonard says.[9] Some women are not whole because they've never been affirmed in their femininity. We all know the story of Sleeping Beauty and the power of the Prince to bring her to life with a kiss. This is a wonderful picture of the power the father has to affirm the feminine within his daughter, and of the ongoing power of the virile prince in her life to appreciate and affirm the beauty and giftedness of the feminine.

I know many women who radiate this feminine energy. They have achieved the balance in uniting feminine spirit and masculine heart. One of them is Maria.

Maria and her husband, a pastor, came to one of our first family life seminars in Germany. Maria was a very beautiful woman, but extremely shy. She told me that she would never be able to speak in public or even be a part of a team. She had very low self-worth and simply couldn't accept herself. I told her my own story. I had had a good father, but he left home to go back to Africa to serve there alone during the Second World War, and he died there. He was not there when I needed him most as a teenager. But at the age of eighteen I found a living relationship with my heavenly Father through his Son. Through this relationship, I have been called and affirmed by my heavenly Father. Every day of my life, I can crawl up on his lap and let myself be loved.

Maria listened and told me of the pain in her own life. I explained that for healing to take place she could do three things: learn to accept herself, receive forgiveness, and forgive those who had wronged her.

Several years later I saw Maria again. I had heard of the fine work she was doing as a pastor's wife. One of the church members told me, "She's the pearl of our village." She was more beautiful than ever, but instead of the shy, "excuse-me-for-breathing-away-your-oxygen" attitude, there was a radiant, confident woman. She gave me a warm hug and said, "Thank you, Ingrid, for showing me years ago the way to my heavenly Father, who loves and accepts me just as I am."

Eva Sanderson, an amazing African Christian who has already made a mark in the political scene of her country, told me her secret. "I've learned to accept myself as I am. What I am today is not what I will be tomorrow. I will get better tomorrow. If others do not accept me, it's their problem and not mine. I'm complete in the Godhead."

I believe that both Maria and Eva radiated "feminine energy" described by Sister Macrina Wiederkehr in her wonderful book *A Tree Full of Angels.* Maria had learned to say yes to the little man inside of her, and this had only enhanced her femininity.

"Feminine energy is powerful," Sister Macrina says, "because it is pure presence—gentle but firm. It is an energy that gives warmth, comfort and spirit simply by its presence. It receives rather than takes. It invites rather than demands. It unfolds rather than overpowers. It finds itself in being rather than in doing. Feminine energy shows her best face in leisure. She doesn't take time. She has time. She has time to be. The world is starving for this energy. It is a part of the fire Christ came to cast on the earth—a slow flame that burns from within and gradually transforms what touches, precisely because it touches rather than clutches."[10]

I believe it is just this energy that sustains life. If women don't have it, it's not because they don't have the potential for it. They may have denied an actual gift that needs to be affirmed.

No Sideways Glance

One of the greatest hindrances to becoming confident is to compare oneself with another person. If I am constantly looking sideways and comparing myself with my friend, my sister, my neighbor, or even a woman of another country, chances are I will be miserable. If I have more confidence in the horizontal dimension of what others think than in the vertical dimension of what God thinks, then it is as if I commit idolatry.

If we care too much about others' opinions of us, we live in the fear of being rejected, hurt, and humiliated. This in turn can go back to earliest childhood, when our desire to be acknowledged, appreciated, and loved was not fully met. So even as adults we try to conceal our weaknesses and become imprisoned by ourselves, thereby creating a vicious cycle. Jealousy and envy, supersensitivity to criticism, shyness and unsureness are the result. In my own battle with shyness, this phrase helped me: "Shyness is really I-ness."

To be subjective, to take everything personally, is as foolish as trying to look at our own eyes. A friend called it the sickness of "ingrown eyeballs." Instead of looking out at the world and seeing things, people, and events as they are, we try to look only inside ourselves. Of course we will be frustrated and miss the whole purpose of vision.

We don't need to compare ourselves with anyone else. "Every sidewise glance is sin," Walter used to tell his counselees. "We don't need the horizontal glance, checking ourselves out with others. We only need the vertical glance, checking ourselves out in God's mirror." Paul made this clear in his letter to the Galatians, "Each one should test (her) own actions. Then (she) can take pride in (herself) without comparing (herself) to somebody else, for each one should carry (her) own load" (Gal. 6:4, 5).

Accepting Limitations

One of the limitations that I have to face as I grow older is that I no longer have the same physical strength I had when I was younger.

When I know that both my time and energy are limited, therefore, I try to use them more wisely. I know that my younger friends can do many jobs much better than I can, when they have been taught and have a vision. Both Walter and I felt that it was wiser to train leaders in our family life seminars than to do them ourselves. I know that my time on this earth is limited, and I want to use it in being faithful to the charge I have been given.

"Every yes is a no," the saying goes. If we say yes to one invitation, it means saying no to another. That is why it is so important to get our priorities straight. What is number one in life? It is good to make a list of priorities every few months to help you make choices about the best use of your time.

My list follows this outline:

1. Be an obedient daughter of my heavenly Father. That means taking time daily to hear the voice of my gentle Shepherd, who never drives me, but quietly leads me.
2. Attend to my family and their needs. Who needs my prayers, my encouragement, my help the most today?
3. Allow time for rest and renewal. Every time I get in an airplane I hear the attendant say, "In the unlikely event of an emergency, put your own oxygen mask on first, and then that of your child." "You are your own best resource," my oldest son told me. "Take care of yourself or you'll have nothing to give." That means such things as exercise, healthful diet, and enough rest.
4. Listing things I know should be done. I used to share my lists with my husband, and his advice usually was, "Have another quiet time and ask the Lord to show you all the things on this list that you do not need to do today." That helped get my priorities straight.

Eleanor Roosevelt has this to say about the painful necessity of accepting one's own limitations:

> Perhaps one of the most difficult things any of us has to do is to be able to say clearly, "This is a limitation in me. Here is a case where, because of some lack of experience or some personal incapacity, I cannot meet a situation. . . ." If you refuse to accept the limitation in yourself, you will be unable to grow beyond this point.
>
> Another ingredient of the maturing process that is almost as painful as accepting your own limitation . . . is learning to accept what other people are unable to give you. You must learn not to demand the impossible or to be upset when you do not get it.[11]

I think many of us women are guilty of living with unrealistic expections, both of ourselves and others. Many of us have a destructive attitude toward ourselves. We are judgmental and harsh, always ready to pounce on ourselves and call ourselves names when we don't live up to self-imposed standards. We also often make pronouncements about others who don't live up to our standards.

Or we're perfectionists. As Norman Wright, family counselor, says to mothers who try to keep a perfect home, "Perfectionism is a thief. It promises rewards but steals joy and satisfaction."[12] A confident woman doesn't waste time apologizing. She does her best at a job and then gets on to the next task. The need to be perfect makes us very sensitive to failure. Our children need to know that we are human. Gertrud, my German mother-in-law, told me in the early days of our marriage, "Nothing in life is one hundred percent."

When we apologize because everything may not be perfect, perhaps it is only false modesty on our part. Or as Oliver Wendell Holmes once put it, "egotism turned wrong side out." The person who apologizes incessantly is like the one who cries "wolf" once too often. True remorse and repentance lose their meaning.

Avoiding Self-Pity

Instead of running into the bedroom and pouting when she is hurt, a confident woman has the courage to speak out, not accusingly, but stating honestly, "I was hurt when you forgot to call that you would be late. I had cooked such a good meal for us because it was a special day and I thought we could celebrate, but you were too busy. Everything is more important that I am." Any hurt that we put into words is already half healed. When a woman tells me that if her husband really loved her, he would know why she was hurt, I have to go to his defense and say, "My dear, he doesn't have a clue unless you tell him. Remember, a baby has the right to be understood without words, but not a grown woman."

The antidote to self-pity is thankfulness. When Ruth Graham was asked whether it wasn't difficult to raise a family of five children when her evangelist husband was traveling all over the globe, she said, "Of course it is, but I would rather have a little of Billy than a lot of some other man."

I found myself sinking into self-pity a few months after Walter died. Everything was too much—the administration of our worldwide ministry, coping with our family finances with four children still in college, and especially the deep hole of personal loneliness in my heart. My youngest daughter was leaving home to study in France for a year, so for the first time since our marriage, my nest was empty.

How could I cope with an empty nest? My friend Reinhild invited me to her home. She had prepared a delicious meal that nurtured not only my body but also my soul. It was one of those times when a mother needs mothering herself. Then she spoke to me firmly but gently. "Look at me, Ingrid. I have no children of my own. A mother never loses her children. Where they are at home, there she can be at home too."

I recalled another time I had been challenged to reject self-pity. As a college student I had failed a nineteenth-century philosophy test and was asked to report to the dean of women. I told her my sob story, how hard I was working—twenty hours of courses and twenty hours of work, and all the other hours for study and just to live. She looked at me and said simply, "Are you sure you're not giving in to self-pity? Go and do better." It was perhaps the most important lesson I learned in college.

The Secret of Acceptance

One Thanksgiving Day I was home alone in the evening. On my favorite radio program Bill Pearce, the host of "Night Sounds," asked us to think of all the things for which we were thankful—our country, our families, home, work, and all the rest. Then he challenged us: "Have you ever stopped to be thankful just for yourself?" As he candidly shared his own struggles with this, I realized that I had never really thanked God for all the work he had done in my creation. I was overcome as I thought of how God had made plans for my life long before I was born, when he chose my grandparents and my parents.

My life began in Old Moshi, a beautiful spot on the slopes of Mount Kilimanjaro, in Tanzania, East Africa. My father was there when I was born. I'm sure he took me in his arms and said, "Look, daughter, at the beautiful world out there." When I was five days old my parents placed me in the arms of Jesus. I was christened in the presence of two thousand African Christians, for it was also the dedication of the new stone church at Mashame, which my father had built. A few days later, it was time to leave Old Moshi and return to the United States.

Our family later settled in the beautiful Ozarks of Missouri, which my parents chose as the best place to raise their large family. I recall one Sunday afternoon when my father explained to me the "miracle of life." He told me that I should begin to pray for the man who would someday be my husband. I did that.

Looking back on my life, I can say two things with gratitude: One is that I have been totally accepted by my heavenly Father, and the other that he called me to be the wife of Walter Trobisch.

Not that it was always easy to keep up with the long steps of my husband.

"To the one who is thankful, ever more and more will be given," Mother Basilea Schlink once wrote. I framed those words and kept them on my desk for many years. Also the thought that there's only one thing that God cannot do, and that is to disappoint those who love him. He gives only the best to those who leave the choice with him. This is the deepest secret of acceptance.

❀ 3 ❀

Discovering Your Place in This World

In his book *Roots,* later serialized on television, Alex Haley gave African-Americans a whole new sense of their history and tradition. When Haley died recently, his epitaph could have been "He gave African-Americans a sense of their roots."

Finding the Good in Your Family Heritage

At a retreat center where I spoke to a women's conference, a state convention of the D.A.R. was in session.

"How can one become a member of the Daughters of the American Revolution?" I asked one of the participants.

"You just have to prove that one of your ancestors fought in the Revolutionary War. And sometimes tracing all the generations back to that time is a very long process," she replied.

I knew I had no chance of being a member of the D.A.R. because my ancestors were all in Sweden at that time. One of them even served in the king's palace as one of his personal guards. A generation later when my grandfather was plowing the virgin prairie soil as a Nebraska homesteader, my husband's grandfather was teaching German to the famous boys' choir of the Thomaskirche in Leipzig, where Bach is buried. And now all this is a part of my children's and grandchildren's heritage.

What do you know about your roots? If your grandparents are no longer alive, try looking up one of the surviving relatives—an aunt, uncle, or cousins. I've tried it, and each time I ask questions I gain a new perspective on my roots. You may find out some scandalous things too. Perhaps that strict great-grandmother you always admired was four months pregnant when she married! We don't really know who we are until we know where we come from. Sometimes this means making peace with the bonds from the past and through forgiveness being set free from the sins of our parents and grandparents.

The *Little House* books by Laura Ingalls Wilder describe the kind of life some of our parents and grandparents lived. Laura's daughter Rose remembers the evenings in their home: "It was the cozy, comfortable hour for all of us. We had had supper, the room was warm, we were alone together, the horses fed and sleeping in the barn, nothing to worry us till tomorrow, and Mama Bess was reading. That was best of all."[1]

Rose's comment reminded me how our family sat around the table after our evening meal and talked. My father read to us from Hurlbut's Bible storybook. Then we held hands around the big table as we sang that simple but wonderful children's prayer, "Jesus, tender Shepherd, hear me." After that we prayed in unison our family prayer, Ps. 67:1–2 (RSV):

> May God be gracious to us and bless us
> and make his face to shine upon us,
> that thy way may be made known upon the earth,
> thy saving power among all nations.

Every Sunday evening we had a program. All of us older children read or recited something. I remember reading out loud the life of David Livingstone and his missionary adventures. We had a little orchestra with flutes and a violin, and my mother accompanied us on the reed organ. Sometimes we all sat in a circle—we called it the family circle—while my father tuned in the radio to Ford's Sunday evening hour. Then he turned off the light and we'd sit in the dark and listen to the music.

A good way to bring back these memories is to look at family albums. For me pictures recall the joy of family reunions, which evoked a grand sense of belonging to a family that was greater than just our own immediate one. Every year the descendants of my great-grandparents would get together the third Sunday in August for a long weekend. The eldest male member of the clan spoke, holding my great-grandfather's walking stick with the gold inlaid handle. He told us how Svante Lind, who had worked in the rocky soil of Sweden, had plowed the first furrow of his Nebraska homestead. He was so overcome with thankfulness that he got down on his knees and picked up a handful of dirt. As it sifted through his hand, he praised God that there wasn't a stone bigger than a pea on this fertile land.

If someone who knows the history of your family is still living, try recording an oral history. Take your tape recorder and ask questions about your past. If they like to write, do what author Elisabeth Elliot found effective with her mother. She bought a hand-size spiral notebook and asked her mother to write the story of her life. Elisabeth says this notebook is one of her most precious possessions. I once asked my mother to do the same thing, and I then typed and duplicated it for the members of her family. It is priceless to us now that we can no longer talk to her.

Walter and I began keeping a journal record of our life together after our wedding. In it we wrote important events and our learning experiences as we lived and worked on three different continents. He wrote most of the text, and I usually illustrated it with sketches and photographs.

As I write this, I see the bookshelf full of our loose-leaf notebooks. When I want to celebrate the birthday of one of our children, I can pull out the notebook in which the birth and the surrounding events are described. "What you have had, no one can take away from you" were the comforting words of Daniel after Walter's death. I realize it anew each time I read one of these notebooks. Someday my grandchildren will be adults, and if they want to go back and trace their roots, they will be able to do it.

A Place of Your Own

The first gift that God gave to Adam and Eve was a place—the garden of Eden. When they lost this God-given garden, they became fugitives. Later their son Cain also was obliged to live the life of a fugitive. That he would never have a place was the worst punishment God could give to Cain (who had killed his own brother).

Jesus too lacked a place in this world: "Foxes have holes and birds of the air have nests, but the Son of Man has no place to lay his head" (Luke 9:58). When we suffer because of a lack of a place, we share this with our Lord. It is Christ himself who is looking for a place of rest within our hearts. If he can find that center within us, we will in turn find a home within him. And through his presence we will become a home for others.

One of the last things Jesus told his disciples was "I go to prepare a place for you" (John 14:3). He who had only the manger and the cross as his places on earth, gave his life to prepare a place for us.

In my travels, I find two kinds of people—those who put too much emphasis on place, and those who downgrade it and don't even see its importance. I believe that many young people are looking for a place, but they don't know where to look. The same is true for women. Those who find a place will become confident and secure and will be able to create a place for others.

Carole Streeter, author of *Women Alone,* has given us this helpful definition of place: "Place is a house or apartment where we live. Place is a neighborhood, a city, a region, a country. Place is a social grouping that is ours, or a relationship that fits. Place is a work in which we feel at home. Place is an aspiration for the future that draws us on to itself. Place is a role that we fill with comfort. Place is the body where we live out who we are. Place is the inner self where we imagine and become."[2]

Place is also land. The Book of Numbers tells the story of the five daughters of Zelophehad, whose father had died while the children of Israel were still in the wilderness. The daughters had entered the Promised Land with their tribe, and they wanted the privilege of owning land, just as other families did. They presented a claim to Moses, who in turn took it before the Lord. He responded, "The claim of the daughters of Zelophehad is good. You must allow them to inherit on the same footing as their father's brothers. Let their father's patrimony pass to them." The laws of the land were changed thereafter so that women could inherit property (Num. 27:1–11).

I understand that today more women than men own land. It may even be a special gift of women to size up property—homes, pieces of land—and see their potentials better than men. One description of the "confident woman" in Prov. 31:16 is this: "She considers a field and buys it; out of her earnings, she plants a vineyard."

From my years in Africa I learned how important the homeland is to Africans. Not only is it a place to be born; it is also a place where they grow up and want to be buried. They say a piece of land never belongs to one person alone but to a vast family, many of whom are dead, a few of whom are living, and a countless number of whom are unborn.

One day I was discussing the issue of place with my son-in-love David Stewart, who as an American consul has lived and worked at U.S. consulates throughout the world. To help me clarify my own thinking, he asked me, "Where do you want to be buried?" A German pastor once counseled his young people to go to the family plot at the cemetery and meditate about their last place on this earth. This would help them get their lives in focus.

Geborgenheit

Geborgenheit is a German word that means a place of safety or security. One Christmas when family members were all together in Austria, my youngest daughter told me that she and her brother Stephen were planning a New Year's retreat for their friends at our home. Ruth was sixteen and Stephen eighteen. Twenty-two of their friends had been invited. "Everything will work out, Mother," she said enthusiastically, "just as long as you remain calm and I remain calm."

We had a very small home, hardly bigger than a weekend cottage, where we had raised our children after we came home from Africa. Ruth insisted there would be room. The young people could just sit on the floor in our living room for the sessions, and our neighbors had offered to share their homes for sleeping arrangements.

"What is your theme?" I asked. "Stephen decided that our theme should be Geborgenheit. That's what all young people are looking for—a place where they are safe." What a good idea, I thought. I remembered asking a young German high school student who was having trouble both with his parents and at school, "Peter, where do you feel safe? Where is your Geborgenheit?"

"The only place I really feel safe is in my old Volkswagen Beetle," he answered without hesitation. "That's the only place that really belongs to me too."

At our first session, Ruth gave each one of us a sheet of paper and asked us to draw the place where we felt sheltered and safe. Several of the youth drew their own single beds with a big pillow and feather bed on top. "That's the only place at boarding school that's really mine," they said. One of my daughters drew the grand piano with a large velvet cover in the music room of her boarding school. "This is where I hide when I want to feel safe," she said. Another youth drew a picture of his mother's hands reaching down to him. Still another drew the family table with the whole family seated around it.

Once when my sister Veda was home on furlough from Africa, where she served as a missionary nurse, she told me the only "place" she had had, that had really belonged to her, was her winter coat. "I loved it. When I put it on, I felt safe and warm," she said. "I wept when I gave it away as I returned to Africa."

A Swiss friend, who had had to flee from her home in Hungary as a teenager, told me about her lifelong search for Geborgenheit, that feeling of being sheltered and safe. She thought her husband should provide it for her, but he too wanted to feel safe and sheltered. Her children couldn't give it to her either. One day she decided that instead of looking for Geborgenheit, she would give Geborgenheit. What happened? Like a boomerang, all that she gave out began to come back to her. "Now my family can't do enough to show me that I am safe and sheltered in their midst," she told me.

How about you? Do you have a place where you experience Geborgenheit? If not, could you begin to create such a place?

The Gift of Hospitality

There is a wonderful story in the Bible about a confident woman who had a gift of hospitality. We don't even know her name. She is simply referred to as the Shunammite. Whenever the prophet Elisha came to her town, she urged him to stay for a meal. Then she asked her husband if they couldn't even make a guest room in their home so that he would have a place to stay: "Let's make a small room on the roof and put in it a bed and a table, a chair and a lamp for him. Then he can stay there whenever he comes to us." When Elisha asked what he could do for her, she replied, "I have a home among my own people" (II Kings 4:8–14). In other words, because she had a place, she could become a place for others. One of the great secrets of the confident woman is that because she knows who she is and where she has come from, she is ready to reach out to others.

I often suggest to women that they learn the art of hostessing themselves. We are foolish if we don't take time, at least a half hour a day, to do what we really want to do and treat ourselves as guests of great honor. For me that means making a cup of tea, using my very nicest cup, and finding a quiet corner where I can play some classical or inspirational music and read something that I really want to savor. Or taking a few minutes to journal, to put down those thoughts that come to me or bits of wisdom that I have heard or read or to arrange photographs and clippings meaningfully to preserve our family's history.

When I bought the lovely old stone farmhouse in Springfield, where I live, the owner, who had also been my grade school teacher, made me promise to do one thing. "Every morning at ten o'clock, Ingrid, I want you to stop what you're doing, get a cup of coffee and either go and sit on the front porch or sit in the swing in the backyard and just listen to the birds. Let your soul be rejuvenated in the beauty of all that is around you." Most of the time I remember to do it.

How I Found My Place

In my early fifties when my husband died, I was at a very vulnerable stage in my life. Ruth, my youngest, had just left home, so I was coping with the empty-nest syndrome. It was a devastating time for me, one that brought me to the crossroads.

Two years later, with my three older children married and the two younger firmly engrossed in their university studies, I decided to pull up roots from our home of eighteen years in Austria and return to the place of my childhood in the United States. Somehow, during my thirty years of glad exile in Africa and Austria, the center of the world for me had always been Springfield, Missouri. From my own experience, I could only underline what Willa Cather, one of America's great writers and a Pulitzer Prize winner, had said: "A person's roots will always be there where a child has spent the years between four and fourteen—providing they were happy years and without undue trauma." Now after my years of living in other continents, I was actually going back to America, and to the Ozarks in particular.

Before I moved, I visited my children Stephen and Ruth, both students in Vienna. We saw a play starring Paula Wessely, one of my favorite Austrian actresses. She played an older woman leaving her Paris apartment to enter a nursing home. Resolutely she packed her suitcases and prepared to leave her "place."

Afterward I talked about the message of the play with my son and daughter.

"But I should go with you to Springfield," my daughter said. "You need help."

"No," I said, "we both have to learn to stand alone. The children must leave their parents, but parents also must leave their children, and then we will find each other again in a new way."

The name of my home is Haus Geborgenheit. I thank God each day for its sturdy, unhewn walls. At the same time, I know that a "geographical place" like this is not possible for many. We must be able to create a "place" anywhere we are.

One of my sisters was visiting me recently. Her husband had just retired after being pastor for thirty-one years in the same parish, where they lived in the church parsonage. "We have no place," she said. "Our home is gone." I could only encourage them to make plans as soon as possible to have their own place, even though it might be only a cabin.

Another good thing I have found out about my place is the joy of taking a daily walk there. Walking is one of the most therapeutic things we can do. Some of my friends go walking in the mall, especially in winter. Others have a favorite park or peaceful neighborhood. The Danish philosopher Søren Kierkegaard advised his troubled niece: "Above all, do not lose your desire to walk. Every day I walk myself into my best thoughts, and I know of no thought so burdensome that one cannot walk away from it."

Finding comfort in my place also requires that I pay attention to orderliness. Because my home is large and my time and strength are limited, I seldom have the luxury of seeing that everything is in apple-pie order. Instead of being depressed by that fact, I have found it a marvelous boost to my confidence to clean up a drawer or a shelf, even though I may not have enough time to clean the whole cupboard. One of my friends suggests thwarting guilt and compulsion by saying, "I don't have much time. But I'm going to give 20 minutes to tidying up this area." The result: a feeling of satisfaction of having done something instead of nothing. It does take time and love to create an orderly place for oneself and others. The French speak of the *tranquillité de l'ordre* (the tranquillity of order), which is all-important if we are to function effectively.

Walter once wrote a prayer letter about place to our friends:

This is the challenge of the hour: to make room by making order. Maybe we should begin by straightening up the things we can see—our drawers, shelves, closets, and also our finances. But above all, we must make order inwardly.

To make order creates new space, but we also need space in which to make order. In a small room where things are heaped up one on top of the other so that we cannot even turn around, we cannot make order. . . .

To turn to God takes room as well. God wants to give it to us. The servant reports, "and still there is room" (Luke 4:22) at God's great banquet table to which all of us are invited.[3]

Our Ultimate Home

My parents worked for many years to pay for the forty-acre farm where five of my brothers and sisters were born and where we were raised. This place is adjacent to where I now live at Haus Geborgenheit. When my father died, my mother took his life insurance money, paid the last thousand dollars of the mortgage, and then gave our home away. It was to be used as a place where tired missionaries could spend their furlough or older years and a place for rest and recreation for Christian workers.

Twice she gave up her earthly place. The first time she followed my father to Africa, where they became pioneer missionaries, a decision that was contrary to the wishes of her parents. Shortly before her fiftieth birthday, she gave up her place again, this time to go to Bolivia, South America, where she served as matron in a large orphanage. As she left the States for her second term of service there, she said good-bye to her children gathered at the airport. "Don't weep," she said. "We have all eternity to spend together, but only a few short years here on earth to be witnesses to those who do not yet know of his love."

The last years of her life were spent in a simple room, one that she had to share with a difficult roommate. I never heard her complain or saw her overcome with self-pity. My sister found a beautiful old desk for the corner of her room. Here she could write letters to her family and friends. "This desk is my hearth," she said when I visited her. I remember one of the last Christmas letters she wrote seated at that desk: "My hands tremble, my legs are unsteady, but my heart is strong and my love for you is unchanging."

She gave away everything she had, so that when it came time to die, all she had to do was die. I was with her the afternoon of her death. Little did either of us expect it to be our last hour together on this earth. A few days earlier, on her ninety-second birthday, she had told me quietly, "You know, Ingrid, I am ready to go anytime." Now as we sat together and drank tea in her little room, she read to me out of the Moravian Texts the word for the day, "Hitherto the Lord has helped us" (1 Sam. 7:12). "That's my life motto," she said. She continued with the prayer, "We are called to love and live fearlessly and be all that we can be." As she was being helped into bed an hour later, she breathed her last.

I remember the afternoon before Walter's unexpected death. We had gone for a walk together in the beautiful Alpine foothills where we lived, having just returned home after three months of missionary travel. "I am homesick, Ingrid, but I don't know for what. I am in the place I love most on this earth, the Lichtenberg, and you are with me."

The next morning, after his usual morning run, Walter prepared a cup of tea for the two of us and brought it to our bedroom. He said to me in German, "My body is trying to tell me something, but I don't understand it." A moment later he took his last breath. He had left his place on earth to go to his ultimate home.

❀ 4 ❀

Using Your Gifts and Developing Skills

One winter a water pipe froze in the top floor of my home. I had been gone for over two months in Africa and Europe. The family who lived in my home during my absence had taken a trip over the weekend, little knowing that an ice storm would keep them from returning as planned. In the meantime, the water poured from the broken pipe through the ceiling of my bedroom, inundating the floor, soaking through to the downstairs den. Thousands of dollars' worth of damage was done before it was discovered. This disruption kept me from working on a writing project.

Instead of meeting the emergency with confidence, I was tempted to panic and to be overcome by the chaos. It was then that I learned how competence dispels confusion. The contractor who came each day to oversee the repairs told me, "Just keep cool." "One thing at a time," the carpenter said. "Don't panic, I can handle it," said the competent painter.

When I learned to keep my eyes looking forward to the finished rooms instead of on the chaos around me, I was able to function. "What are your directions for today, Lord?" I would ask in my quiet time. Then I would pray for grace to obey those directions. I could take only the next indicated step and see a faint light at the end of the tunnel. After the job was done, I had a beautiful new interior. I am very grateful.

The man who cleaned the carpets and furniture did an expert job. When I congratulated him on his work, he said, "You need to have the assurance that you're the best in this business. Otherwise you won't make it. One of my friends who does this work too always underbids because he doesn't have enough self-esteem. Now he's bankrupt. So you've got to believe in yourself, even when it comes to cleaning carpets."

The two women who did the wallpapering had the same attitude. They were confident because they were competent.

Identifying Your Areas of Competence

One of my friends is a very good organist. "Are you a confident woman, June?" I asked when I met her recently at a bookstore. "Are you competent?"

"That depends on whether or not I have practiced," she answered.

Have you ever made a list of all the things you can do well? This is a helpful exercise, and you can do it either alone or with some of your closest friends. You might also ask your family members what they think you can do well.

I asked my sister Eunie, who lives next door to me, what activities she felt competent in. "I'm good at grocery shopping," she said. I could verify that, for she can stretch food dollars better than anyone I know and still cook wonderfully balanced and tasty meals. "Oh, yes, I'm good at packing for trips, at choosing the essential and leaving at home the nonessential." "What about your nursing?" I asked her. "Yes, I feel competent there. I know how to make people feel comfortable and allay their fears." I've heard many of her former patients praise her nursing skills in helping them recover from painful operations.

An example of a competent and thus confident woman is Roberta Hestenes, called to be the first woman president of Eastern College in St. Davids, Pennsylvania. She describes herself as a

Christian feminist. When asked how that is similar to or different from a secular feminist, she replied, "I call myself an evangelical Christian feminist, which means I am a person who believes the Scriptures, when properly interpreted and applied, teach the full partnership of men and women in the church, the family, and society. . . . There are still places of deep resistance and hostility toward changing roles for women, but I think on the whole there is more to be encouraged about than to be discouraged about."

When asked what advice she would have for an evangelical woman who feels called to leadership, this was her answer: "She should become a person of prayer and spiritual discernment, so that she really is seeking to minister out of her desire to be Christ's person and obedient to the will of God. She should also be willing to take risks, including the risk of not being approved of by everybody."[1]

Learning New Skills

Maybe you've never learned how to swim. I have many older friends who did not learn as children and who even had great fear of water. But they had the courage to enroll in an adult swimming class at the Y. Now they are competent swimmers.

Learning a new language is something that one is never too old to do. What a joy to begin to understand words in another culture. My oldest brother was teaching a class in Spanish as part of a continuing education program in the Tucson schools. He told me that most of his ambitious pupils were over sixty-five. Every time he had class he took the roll. One week he missed an Edith Johnson who had been a regular attendant. When he asked if anyone knew why she hadn't come, her acquaintance said to my brother, "Oh, Mrs. Johnson died last week." She was eighty-three, and until the last week of her life she was improving her Spanish!

Computer skills, bookkeeping and accounting, nursing skills— all can be learned at vocational schools in evening classes. My friend and I just took a seven-week course in watercolor painting.

Our teacher said that it's not enough to look; we must also see. As we learned to see values of light, mix colors, and then put them on paper, we felt a renewing and cleansing of the mind. It took an effort for both of us to clear our schedules so that we could take the class, but we're on our way now toward competence in this area instead of just wishful thinking. The journey is its own reward.

"I feel competent, but not always confident," a friend told me recently. "I can do wifing, mothering, hostessing, cooking, teaching." Mary is the mother of seven children, whom she teaches at home through the fourth grade. She has a great desire to learn German, so once a week, she puts everything aside and does just that.

Another friend wants to learn to play the flute better. Her children are both in high school, so she has more free time than when they were younger. She works with a good teacher to improve her skills. I think of a family therapist, now in her fifties, who is taking piano lessons again after many years of interruption. "What joy and satisfaction I get from doing this," she said. "And every week, I'm getting better."

Competence comes from practice. "You can study all the books you want to about carpentry," said a friend of mine, "but until you do it over and over again, you will never be competent. You learn the most from your own mistakes."

I believe that competence also comes from hard work. It has often been a comfort to me as a writer to know that "Hard writing makes easy reading." I learned early on that when I write, I have to set aside a regular time each day and set a goal for each day. Then I write, whether I feel like it or not. Most writing is not inspiration but perspiration.

"Learn to do something well," I often tell women at retreats. We all need to feel competent in some areas.

The wives of my Austrian farmer neighbors were competent women. They were the ones who milked, fed, and cared for dairy cattle. They could drive tractors and help bring in the harvest.

They were all good cooks and seamstresses and could do complicated handwork, like knitting, crocheting, and embroidery. One of them even gave me a tablecloth that she had spun and woven herself from homegrown flax. Besides that they were active in teaching their children and supervising their homework. None of these women seemed to have an identity crisis. I believe it is because they knew their mountain farms could not run without them.

What are things that make a woman feel happy and confident? Baking bread, playing a musical instrument, sewing a garment, driving a car, weaving a rug, performing surgery, handling investments. Every new skill that a woman learns adds to her ability to tackle new tasks.

The Father's Contribution to His Daughter's Competence

A father has a lot to do with his daughter's competence. If American women are good drivers, it is often because their fathers taught them not only how to drive but also how to take care of a car.

When you study the life history of famous women stage artists, you will find that very often these women were encouraged by their fathers when they were young. It was the father who helped his daughter overcome fear.

Fathers are often the trainers and coaches of famous women athletes. I saw an interview with the father of one of the best women basketball players of the season. She was only five feet four. Her father said, "I told her to act like a lady when she was off the court but to play like a man when she was on court."

Another report was about female tennis stars who began to be famous already in their early teens. The commentator said that all these girls had one thing in common: They each had a father who was their backer and encourager and who taught them to keep on trying harder.

"You gain strength, courage, and confidence by every experience in which you really stop to look fear in the face," said Eleanor Roosevelt. "You must do the thing you cannot do."

Eleanor lost her father (who was a brother of Teddy Roosevelt) just before her tenth birthday. She had promised her father that she would grow up to be a woman he could be proud of. After his death, Eleanor dedicated herself to continue the causes her father believed in. "She did what many fatherless women have done: She validated and extended her father's existence through her own. This was true of Bess Truman and Rosalynn Carter, who lost their fathers through death, and Jacqueline Kennedy and Nancy Reagan, who lost their fathers through divorce."[2]

Another interesting example of a woman who sought to re-create in her life work the longed-for image of her dead father is Barbara Streisand. She devoted years to making the film *Yentl*, in which the father is warm and kind, wise and compassionate—the kind of father every woman would like to have. The woman in the film then keeps him alive by carrying on the love and reverence for books and learning he had passed on to her.

In the life stories of successful, competent women who may not have had an encouraging father, we can often find the presence of a male mentor. Gail Sheehy in her book *Pathfinders* gives this definition of such a mentor: "Most pathfinders describe at least one strong model who influenced them during childhood . . . who offered some guiding principles, who helped them to make a leap of growth instead of falling into a developmental ditch. . . . This person could be a teacher, a coach, a doctor, or a sibling, uncle, grandparent, or a friend, all the way up to a full-fledged mentor. . . . A mentor is a trusted friend and counselor, usually from ten to twenty years old, who endorses the apprentice's dream and helps in a critical way to guide him or her toward realizing it."[3]

Competence in Working with Men

"What qualities do you look for in the women who are your co-workers?" I asked my neighbor Galen, one of Springfield's leading oncologists, as we chatted in his home.

"Doctors are very insecure people," he said. "Women have a resourcefulness that most men don't have, so I want the women on my staff to use both their resourcefulness and leadership qualities. I want them to be accepting, not critical, of me. I also want them to be accepting of the other women working in our office. If not, they make life miserable for all of us—both men and women."

A word is in order here about competence in dealing with our physicians. A woman who has a hysterectomy or mastectomy is vulnerable and needs to be confident and have confidence in her physician. A friend of mine had major surgery, which involved the removal of her uterus and ovaries. I went to visit her and she told me of her talk with her surgeon before the operation. She said that because of her long struggle with MS and her inability to move her body quickly, she was extremely vulnerable, even to words spoken by her surgeon when she was under anesthesia. She asked him not to make any negative remarks about her body during surgery, knowing that the physical wounds would be difficult enough to cope with after the operation without also having wounds in the unconscious.

One woman I know who is competent in working with men is my friend Reinhild. As the director of a high school in Mannheim, Germany, where the majority of her colleagues are men, she was always impressed that the men were very eager to hear her word of approval. They seemed to welcome it even more than their female counterparts.

In my own experience in working with various publishing houses throughout the world, I have been impressed by the number of competent women who are on the team as editors and secretaries. Above all they seem to create an atmosphere which made men feel comfortable and which gets things done.

I asked a friend who works as an investor what he expected from the women on his staff. His answer, "Professional competence without a 'feminist agenda.' Women are nurturing and they have innate people skills which we men don't always have. It's not a question of competing with one another, but of completing and complementing one another." "I have learned to work with difficult men," one professional woman told me. Because of that, there was a sense of peace in her office. A woman who is not confident in herself can be a destructive influence both for other women and for the men in her life.

Creativity and Competence

We cannot live in a vacuum. We have to express our being by creating. Creativity follows being. Rollo May, a psychotherapist, says in his book *The Courage to Create* that courage is essential for the creative act. It is not the absence of despair, rather it is the capacity to move ahead in spite of despair. We should not confuse it with rashness. Courage comes from the same stem as the French word *coeur*, meaning "heart." According to Webster, creativity is "the process of making, of bringing into being."

In other words, if you have an idea for a story but never write it down, then you have never created. When I sketch and paint, both watercolors and oil, I find that I am totally absorbed, wholly involved—spirit, mind, and body. It is almost as if a deep cleansing takes place within me. I can experience in my own being the truth of Rollo May's statement: "Genuine creativity is characterized by an intensity of awareness, a heightened consciousness."[4]

Many women in the Ozarks, where I live, are competent in crafts: needlework, quilting, fine metalwork, porcelain painting. I am amazed at what their competence, which comes from long years of practice, does to strengthen their confidence. Their healthy self-confidence causes many other troubles (some of them psychological) to take care of themselves.

Lifelong Learning

In her autobiography, written when she was eighty-six, Rose Kennedy quoted from a book that she said she was reading "to further her education."

When my own mother at the age of fifty took a mission assignment in Bolivia, she had to learn Spanish. She wrote to her children that it was the tenth language she had studied in her life, "and the easiest," she added.

To celebrate her seventieth birthday, she came to visit us in Austria. Every day she took time to learn and perfect her German. When she went to live at Augustana Home in Minneapolis at the age of eighty-five, her great joy was to spend several hours each week studying Spanish with a friend there. Her mind was always thirsty to learn new things. Her grandchildren were hard put when they met up with her expertise in Scrabble.

Up until the week she died, at the age of ninety-two, she read books—at least one every two weeks. When I was with her, she would read to me out of her current book. I teased her and said, "You never had time to read to me when I was little, but now you're making up for it." She went through the daily papers from cover to cover and watched the evening news. She followed the political scene carefully, and in a presidential election year was informed about each candidate.

A woman who is constantly learning new things and who is skilled in at least one will be both confident and competent. She knows that she can do something well and is not threatened by others, nor by what others say. This is especially true in the professional world. Her walk and talk betray her confidence (or lack of it). If she is not knowledgeable about something, she is not afraid to ask.

The confident woman is not intimidated by reproaches, nor does she complain when things do not go her way. She learns how to cope and adapt to that which may not be in her way of thinking.

A friend whose elderly husband seems to be very limited in his vision of the world and its needs, while she has a generous, open heart, wrote to me, "Sometimes life feels like living in a square box, and any way I turn I run into walls; but, thank God, there is no lid on the box. I can look up, and that keeps me going."

I am grateful that both confidence and competence do not come from my limited stores of being. The apostle Paul said, "I can do everything through him who gives me strength" (Phil. 4:13, NIV). We can draw both our confidence and competence from the deep springs of God's Word, where we read in 2 Cor. 3:4, 5 (NIV): "Such confidence as this is ours through Christ before God. Not that we are competent in ourselves to claim anything for ourselves, but our competence comes from God."

II

Confident in Your Relationships

❀ 5 ❀

Living Confidently with Other Women

How can I live confidently with other women? If I am not comfortable with the women in my family and in my work, how can I expect to be comfortable and confident with the men in my life?

A hairdresser beginning a new job said to me, "I appreciate working here. If the owner doesn't like something I do, she tells me right away. All of my colleagues are the same way. That way I know they don't talk behind my back, and I feel both comfortable and confident here."

Let's back up and look at the first relationship we had with another woman, namely with our own mother.

Mother–Daughter Relationships

I grew up as the eldest, very sensitive, daughter of a practical, down-to-earth mother. She had grown up in a family with three big brothers—all of them baseball players. She was a good athlete too and won every footrace she ran. Her particular favorites were puppy dogs and little boys. She had an amazing lack of self-pity and taught us, in the words of my sister, "cheerfulness, thankfulness and hard work." Eunie continued in a memorial tribute to our mother,

She modeled how to be respectful and helpful to others. She instilled in me an eagerness to learn and to appreciate the world around us. She urged me to "try harder" and never give up. She also taught the importance of a healthy diet and she worked hard in her kitchen and garden to provide that. She instructed me in cooking, baking, cleaning, washing, ironing and mending. But most of all, Mother taught me to love the Lord and His Word."[1]

One summer evening when I was twelve I was helping my mother take down the clothes. We had a clothesline strung from the large hickory tree in our backyard to the two oak trees and back again. We worked in harmony as we took down a large white sheet, folded it together, and laid it in the clothes basket. Then, instead of taking down the next sheet, she stopped, put her arms around me, and gave me a hug. I was taken by surprise, but I remember that it felt good. Often in the years to come, when we were separated by continents, I was warmed by the memory of that unexpected hug.

I once told my sister Veda when we were talking about our relationships with our parents and as sisters, "I can never remember sitting on Mother's lap." "Of course you can't," Veda said, "I came along and pushed you off." There are nineteen months between our birth dates.

Often I have spoken with women who have "mother problems," who have felt rejected since even before birth, whose mothers have kept them at arm's distance because they had been kept that way by their own mothers. "I didn't mean to keep you out," one mother said to her daughter. "I just didn't know you wanted to come in." I have to tell these women, "If you do not like your mother, your father, then you will also not like yourself." Sometimes a whole process of inner healing has to take place here.

To know and then accept my family of origin has a lot to do with my own self-acceptance. Sometimes I need to forgive a wrong that has been done to me. That includes the feeling of emptiness that comes from a lack of love and understanding as I may have perceived it.

Once when I was visiting in the home of my eldest daughter Katrine she invited me to take part in a women's bible study group that she was hosting. It was a Saturday morning, as I recall, and her husband, David, as well as the other fathers had agreed to take care of the children so that their wives could have an undisturbed time together. As we talked about forgiveness, one of the women suggested that we tell our most hurting experience with our own mother or a mother-figure. After telling our stories, we each made a conscious act to forgive that person. Tears were shed and much healing took place in that sheltered atmosphere. A childhood memory came to my mind that had always blocked the flow of true feeling toward my mother, and for which I had secretly reproached her. How good it was to get it out and have a clean slate. Then I listened as my own daughter spoke out her painful experiences at boarding school. "I felt forsaken all those years away at school," she said.

When my mother had to be hospitalized, a friend and I went to visit her. She told my friend as my back was turned, "Ingrid was always a good big sister to her younger siblings." I turned around and said, "Mother, you are now eighty-two. Why did you never tell me that? It would have helped me so much all these years." "Because I didn't want you to get proud" was her answer. That day when I kissed her good-bye, I heard her say for the first time, "Ingrid, I love you." Perhaps she had never heard these words from her own mother.

More than once I have had the privilege of being a substitute mother for a younger woman who had inadequate mothering. I remember having this great "mother hunger" myself when I was overseas. I talked it over with Mother Amalia, who together with her husband, Klaus Hess, acted as spiritual mentors for Walter and me. Mother Amalia listened quietly as I told her of my pain. She had no great words of comfort but simply put her arms around me and let me weep on her shoulder.

Having healthy relationships with our married daughters and our daughters-in-law often depends on our own attitudes. I was quite surprised on the evening before our wedding in Mannheim, Germany, when "Mutti," my mother-in-law-to-be, stood up and said that she wanted to make an announcement to the wedding party. I listened as she looked at me and said, "I hereby give up the first place in the life of my son Walter and give it to Ingrid." I knew that Walter and his mother had a good relationship and enjoyed to the fullest any time they could spend together. She spent every Sunday evening writing to her children, and they kept in touch with her. Mutti later told me how she had suffered because of the attitude of her mother-in-law. Mutti did not want her daughters-in-law to go through the same experience.

Someone has said that the mother-in-law problem is created because two women are in love with the same man. Unless there has been a leaving of father and mother, there can be no real cleaving in marriage. I know from experience after having become a mother-in-law five times over how difficult it is to let go of our sons and daughters. I like to use the terms *daughter-in-love* and *son-in-love*. That means loyalty and affirmation of these new family members. I want to give them the feeling that I'm on their side and that there will be no talking behind their backs.

Miss Lillian, Jimmy Carter's mother, once said that she made a point of never making a negative remark about one of her daughters-in-law. Walter often said, "Every negative remark we make is a prayer to the devil."

Mothering Our Own Mothers

Today many women in midlife have to mother their own mothers as these women become older and increasingly dependent. This role reversal can be difficult, and it demands a good deal of unselfishness and love. In her comic strip *For Better or for Worse,* Lynn Johnston illustrated how she helped her parents to move out of their home into a smaller place. When her husband,

Phil, came to pick her up, he said to her, "Strange how the roles have been reversed, isn't it. We're becoming parents to our parents." "I know," she answered, "and I'm not ready to stop being the child."[2]

Many of my best friends have lived through this stage. Reinhild wrote to me after caring lovingly for her mother for over a decade, "This morning Mother died peacefully in my arms. I have no regrets."

I watched Elisabeth, my German editor, faithfully care for her mother. During the last months of her life, Elisabeth's mother needed round-the-clock care. Elisabeth was able to do much of her editorial work at home. She arranged for volunteers and home nurses to help with her mother's care when she had to be in the office. I never heard her complain when she had to give up well-earned vacations with exciting trips. Each time I saw her, Elisabeth had a radiant face and no self-pity as she enabled her mother to die in dignity.

It was both a burden and a joy for my sisters and me to be intimately involved with our mother's care during the last years of her life. The secret was not to be pressured by the thought that everything had to be done that normally would have been on our schedules. It is good now to look back and have no regrets, to realize that these months and years of care giving are but a passing stage in the whole circle of life. The best rule here is the Golden Rule—to give the care that we ourselves would like to receive.

Sibling Sisters

The relationship of sibling sisters is special. Anne Lindbergh describes a day with her sister after she has been alone for a week on an island:

> We wake in the same small room from the deep sleep of good children. . . . We run bare-legged to the beach. . . . The morning swim has the nature of a blessing to me, a baptism, a rebirth

to the beauty and wonder of the world. We run back tingling to
hot coffee on our small porch. . . .

We wash the dishes lightly to no system, for there are not
enough to matter. We work easily and instinctively together,
not bumping into each other as we go back and forth about
our tasks. We talk as we sweep, as we dry, as we put away, discussing a person or a poem or a memory. And since our com-
munication is more important to us than our chores, the
chores are done without thinking."[3]

When I think of the relationship of sisters, I think of words
like these: speaking the same language—sometimes words aren't
even necessary—working together, bossing (but no one minds),
cheering, approving, correcting, forgiving, comforting, relaxing,
but above all trusting and understanding. Is there any closer relationship? I think of my sisters as my next of kin. When they are
also best friends, that is a gift indeed.

But what if that is not the case? There can be a strong sense of
sibling rivalry. One young woman told me when I asked how she
honestly felt about her big sister, "There are times when I feel
like sinking my claws into her." She admitted this had a lot to do
with jealousy. Her big sister had a closer circle of friends, was a
better athlete, and seemed to delight in putting her little sister
down.

Often this time of rivalry takes care of itself as the two become
older and become allies instead of rivals. When my father died
and again when my husband died, I found the greatest comfort
in being with my sisters. It was the pain of loss that drew us together in a special way.

In a television interview, Anne Morrow Lindbergh recalled
the terrible experience of the kidnapping of her child and the resulting lack of privacy that caused them to flee to England. Her
husband warned her about writing any letters that she wouldn't
mind seeing blasted across the front page of the *New York Times*.
In spite of the warning, she insisted, "I had to write letters to my
sisters. It was like breathing."[4]

In *Blackberry Winter* Margaret Mead has written this about sisters in old age: "Sisters is probably *the* most competitive relationship within the family, but once the sisters are grown, it becomes the strongest relationship. On the whole, sisters would rather live with each other than anyone else in their old age."[5]

The Gift of Friends

Jesus said in John 15:15, "No longer do I call you servants . . . but I have called you friends" (RSV). After experiencing this friendship with God, my next most meaningful gift is having earthly friends. They are my encouragers, cheering me on when I have to climb high mountains or go through difficult places. Friends are my comforters when I fall; they help me get up again and see past the struggles to the ultimate goal. They are my sounding board and give me feedback. They listen carefully when I tell my story and offer quiet nuggets of wisdom that give light for the next step. I know I can count on them always to be there when I need them. I've told you of some of my friends— Reinhild and Elisabeth—but there are many others, both women and men. These friends accept me just the way I am, but like Christ, they don't leave me that way. They help me to break out of my walls of self-pity and discouragement. I call them my circle of lovers.

A friend is someone to whom I do not have to explain myself. Such a friendship offers unspeakable comfort. Friendships can also be redemptive, for friends can act as mediators of God's presence and invite us into the embrace of God's grace.

In some friendships, we must do more giving. It is then that we are called to become midwives for whatever God is bringing to birth in our friends. In other friendships, we are more on the receiving end. It is important to balance our friendships so that sometimes we are the givers and other times we are the receivers.

In our circle of friends we also need a confidante. According to the dictionary, a confidante is someone to whom you can entrust your secrets. I would prefer to replace the word *confidante* with *Doula,* an anthropological term coined by Dana Raphael that means "someone who mothers the mother" or who takes care of the care giver.[6] This is an accepted part of society in all cultures except our Western one.

In most African tribes, after the birth of a baby a mother is celebrated and exempt from the hard work of keeping house for a certain period of time. She is to spend time and be bonded with her baby, to be "fattened" so that she will have strength to breast-feed her child and after an appropriate time of rest take up her other duties again.

I find this concept sadly lacking in our society. In former days, it was the grandmother who could be the doula for her daughter, but today's grandmothers are often in the work force themselves and perhaps have no vision for what this could mean for the future of the family. Maybe we need to start courses for doulas, people not necessarily related to the mother or care giver.

I was asked to speak to young mothers in a local congregation near Springfield. During the morning session, as I spoke and answered questions from the group, the older women of the parish watched the children and cooked a delicious meal for the younger women. After the meal the young mothers took their children and went home, and then it was the older women's turn to listen. This congregation was full of young families, which was not surprising when one considered the care and sensitivity they were shown.

When I suggest to older women that they "adopt" a young mother in their neighborhood and help her so that she can come up for air once a week, they often protest, saying that they would feel meddlesome even to suggest this. Then I tell them about what my friend Reinhild and other doulas along the way have done for me.

In Titus 2:3, 4 we read Paul's instructions to older women to "teach what is good, train the younger women to love their husbands and children . . . to be kind." When this word is taken seriously, it can have far-reaching consequences. One of them is more competent and fulfilled mothers. The younger woman has someone to cheer her on and affirm her in exercising the greatest profession in the world, that of being a people maker.

The Mother Heart of the Father God

I hadn't thought much about God's mothering of us until one of our spiritual mentors, Klaus Hess, who was then in his eighties, talked to us about it. He said that both motherliness and fatherliness are attributes of God. The older and more mature we become, the more "motherly" a man can be, just as a woman can become fatherly.

"Could you tell me your favorite Bible passage?" I asked Walter one day. Without hesitation, he quoted Isa. 66:13, "As a mother comforts her child, so I will comfort you" (NIV). It was in the foxholes of Russia, when the German doctor told the troops that they had only twenty-four hours to live before they could expect to freeze to death or be captured by the Russians that Walter experienced this word personally. The Father God compares himself with a mother comforting her child.

Another motherly quality of God is that he nourishes us. He is likened to a nursing mother in Isaiah 9. He certainly nurtured and nourished his people on their forty-year trek through the wilderness. Every day except the Sabbath they were given fresh manna. When they complained about the monotony of the bread, the motherly God even provided them with quails. Haven't you seen mothers doing the same thing, trying to please the taste buds of their cantankerous children?

One spring I escaped for a few days to my little house in the forest in the Ozark Mountains. I had been going through a wilderness both spiritually and physically. As I sat in the clearing behind my cabin, enjoying the first sights and sounds of spring in the Ozarks, a covey of quails swooped down at my feet. They busied themselves with a search for food in the matted grass and dry leaves left over from winter. I watched in breathless fascination as if through them the Lord had delivered this message: "I have given you manna for your journey, but there are some nice surprises ahead in your life." I felt greatly loved by this gentle sign from the motherly heart of God.

When Elijah was in hiding at the brook east of Jordan, God sent ravens to bring him bread and meat in the morning and bread and meat in the evening (1 Kings 17:6). Later on, after a great victory, Elijah had to flee for his life. He sat under a broom tree and prayed that he might die. "I've had enough, Lord. Take my life." God didn't argue with him but did a very motherly thing. He sent an angel, who touched him and baked him a cake. Elijah ate and drank and then lay down. A second time God sent the angel to him, who touched him again and said, "Get up and eat, for the journey is too much for you" (1 Kings 19:7). With new strength, Elijah was able to continue his ministry.

In my study I ponder the replica of a stained glass window from a European cathedral. It is hanging on the west window so that the light streams through it. An angel is shown holding up the roof, which is a section of a vaulted ceiling. The angel, bracing herself firmly to do it, does not have the Atlas quality of a strong man straining all his muscles to lift a heavy weight. Rather she is a woman poised in action to do her job.

My friend Reinhild, who gave me this beautiful gift for my home, explained its symbolism: "It's to honor mothers," she said, "also God's motherliness. Often it's the mother who holds up the roof, who gives her family that feeling of being sheltered, of being covered, of being safely under the roof."

We are secure under God's protection, as we read in Ps. 91:1, 4a: "He/she who dwells in the shelter of the Most High will rest in the shadow of the Almighty. . . . He will cover you with his feathers and under his wings you will find refuge." If I had to choose only one verse, this would be my favorite. Once more it shows the mother heart of the Father God.

Being covered and sheltered evokes intense feelings of comfort. It contains elements of both motherliness and fatherliness. I knew that I could love my future husband when he spread a blanket over my cold feet after a wintry ride on his motorcycle. I have watched his sons doing the same thing. I feel safe when I am covered with an afghan that my sister made for me or with the quilt my grandmother made for me. It's a little threadbare now after serving in our homes on three continents, but it's still a symbol of her love.

In the years since Walter's death, I have had times of unspeakable sadness. Then I have sometimes felt an invisible hand covering me, and I am strangely comforted by this motherly gesture of my heavenly Father.

The Kiga tribe in East Africa gives God the name of Biheko, which means "a God who carries everyone on his back." In this tribe, only mothers and older sisters carry children on their backs. To portray Biheko, one of their artists made a wooden carving of a man carrying on his back a child with an adult face and in his arms a weaker child. This carving is a symbol of the God who takes care of human beings with the tender care of a mother, the God who said, "Even to your old age and gray hairs I am he, I am he who will sustain you. I have made you and I will carry you" (Isa. 46:4, NIV).

❀ 6 ❀

The Confident Single Woman

One of my best friends died recently. Her name was Anneliese, and she lived close to Karlsruhe, Germany. For over forty years we had corresponded, and on rare occasions we were able to be together. Although she didn't speak English, she dared to fly across the Atlantic and visit me at Haus Geborgenheit in Springfield. I saw her in her home three weeks before she died, her body ravaged by cancer. "Today I don't feel any pain," she said, "for the joy that you have come."

Anneliese was a competent professional. She was the head of her department at a sewing machine factory. Her job was to train young women to demonstrate the machines at trade fairs throughout the world. She served as both a role model and mentor for her apprentices.

Like so many young women of her day in Germany, Anneliese had been engaged to be married, but her fiancé was killed in World War II. She didn't often talk of her sorrow, except to say that she had learned to accept her singleness. Her greatest grief was giving up motherhood. This sadness was turned into joy when over the years twelve of her married friends asked her to be godmother to their children. She took this call very seriously and became both a spiritual mother and a friend to each one of her godchildren, and that included one of our sons. "I shall never forget her telephone calls, even across the Atlantic," he said.

"Somehow I have the feeling she'll still be making calls from her heavenly home."

I missed her call yesterday. It would have been my fortieth wedding anniversary, and not once in these forty years had she forgotten to write or call. She was also a good friend to Walter, and he often said, "When Anneliese retires from her job, we will invite her to spend longer periods of time in our home." I believe that men liked her because she understood and affirmed them.

What was her secret? Because she was an important person to herself, she could pour out her life for others. She didn't waste time on self-pity. She knew who she was and accepted her gifts and her limitations. She had also allowed that "little man" inside her to develop without losing her femininity. The result was an indefinable "feminine energy" that radiated from her. She was a surrogate mother and grandmother for my children and grandchildren. Her death has left a great hole but many good memories in their hearts.

Becoming a Whole Person

You are a woman alone. Maybe you have never married, or you are no longer married. You're a divorcée, a single mother, or a widow. Maybe you're mourning a broken friendship with a man that has left you with the taste of ashes in your mouth. In spite of your efforts, there's still an emptiness, a vacuum in your life.

You wonder why singleness has come to imply being alone rather than being a whole person. That is what I want to explore in this chapter—how we can come to wholeness in both our relationship to ourselves and to others.

Some women think that only if they are married will all things be in balance. "Marriage is not a hospital for sick hearts," Hermann Oeser once wrote. Nor is it "a shoulder to lean on," as a French woman confided to me when she confessed that she had made a wrong choice and married too soon. Being single successfully means to be a whole person.

Wholeness comes when we are affirmed not only in our femininity but also in our masculinity. This was a long journey for me. A year after my husband's death, I visited Esther Bradley, a friend in Dublin, Ireland. Esther, a physician and counselor as well as wife and mother, said to me as we talked about grief, singleness, and remarriage, "Ingrid, you've got to stop the bleeding points. Allow yourself to be strong and creative, to plan and structure, to say just the right word at the right time, to think logically and to show others the way, for that is your calling from God. You have said yes to your femininity. Now learn to say yes to that gentle but strong Daniel in your heart."

We also talked about the temptation to think that marriage or remarriage is the way to wholeness. An elderly woman who lost her beloved husband remarried in the first year of her widowhood. She confessed to her daughter that she had made a mistake and said poignantly, "There's nothing lonelier than being married to the wrong man."

Becoming a whole person takes courage, but it brings rich rewards. There is an Irish fairy tale about a mortal on a fairysteed who went hunting with the fairies. He had to decide whether he wanted the fairy horse to become large enough to carry a normal-size man or to remain fairy size and for he himself to shrink. He chose to become of fairy size. He rode merrily with the fairy king until he came to a wall so high he feared his tiny horse could not carry him over. But the fairy king said to him, "Throw your heart over the wall, then follow it!" So he rode fearlessly at the wall, and with his heart already bravely past it, he went safely over.

This legend has a message for the confident woman. If we would win success in anything, we mustn't give up when we come to a wall that bars our way—be it our loneliness or our singleness. Hesitation can mean defeat. In faith we must throw our hearts over the barrier and then follow confidently, like a good horse and its rider.

In reaching for wholeness, a single woman also needs both recognition and belonging, and we turn now to these.

The Need for Recognition

Single people are the fastest-growing "family type" in America. In 1992 there were about sixty-five million single adults in the United States, 37 percent of the population. By the year 2000, according to the U.S. Census Bureau, single adults may make up 50 percent of the total adult population.

"We want to be taken seriously," says Carole Streeter in her book *Women Alone.* "If other people do not take us seriously, we have a hard time doing so. Conversely, if we do not take ourselves seriously, it is unlikely that anyone else will either."[1]

I learned from my friend Anneliese that one cannot "be" in a vacuum. We express our being by creating, so that creativity is a necessary sequel to being. That takes courage, which is not the absence of despair but the capacity to move ahead in spite of despair.

Two of the greatest problems Christian single women often face are their invisibility and the uncertainty they feel about themselves. If one is not acknowledged, then it is but a small step to think, "I do not matter" or even "I do not exist." Guilt and a lack of self-worth are likely to follow.

I believe that doing quietly what we have to do is recognition enough. After finishing college and a special training course for overseas missionaries, I made plans to go to West Africa to serve as a teacher in French-speaking Cameroon. Before my departure I was interviewed by a young woman reporter from the local paper. She wanted to do a story for her weekly feature "Career Girl." After recounting the adventures of the "vivacious, titian-haired missionary, twenty-two years of age," she concluded: "Here is one field, girls, that we can guarantee is not overcrowded."

I was able to visit my father's grave in Dar-es-Salaam, Tanzania, for the first time. More than a decade later, I visited my sister Veda, who was head nurse at the Iambi Leprosarium, where five hundred patients were cared for in Christian love. In my journal at that time I wrote this tribute to her and the wonderful single women like her scattered at lonely mission stations throughout the world:

> These noble single workers—how shall I describe them? They're women, all of them; but they're supposed to do the work of men. They're women; but they can't afford to be weak. They must hide their feelings behind an armor of self-protection. They have to handle jeeps, driving through roads where there's no bottom, or cowpaths where there are no markers. They have to hoist boxes and barrels, build outstations, deliver babies, organize leprosy patients, perform a hundred tasks for which they may not be fitted. But if they fail somewhere along the way, they are subjected to merciless criticism. They are here because they have been obedient to God's call, and he has entrusted them with this great task. It's proof to me of God's power as I see the work of these noble ones.

The Need to Belong

To be single successfully we must become whole persons. That means dealing with aloneness. I was greatly comforted in my life as a single to know that "God sets the lonely in families" (Ps. 68:6, NIV). Other translations read, "God makes a home for the lonely." He does this for me through good friends, members of my extended family, church groups or interest groups, and helping me to reach out to those who need my help. Just to know that God is concerned for the lonely makes me feel loved.

"I don't need a singles' group," said one of our single co-workers recently. "I need to be included in groups where there are both singles and couples. This helps me keep the right perspective." My secretary, not yet married, was my dialogue partner at one of the family life retreats my coworkers and I led in Salzburg, Austria. After the retreat, Elisabeth thanked me for including her and said, "It's true, I may be missing some of the joys that couples have, but I'm also spared a lot of pain. I didn't know how difficult it is to be married."

A young woman teacher said, "Married people sometimes tell me that I should be thankful because I am free and don't have all the responsibilities for home and family that they have. How can I let them know that what I really want is to be needed?"

When I shared this thought with Katrine, whose home has been open for singles from around the world, she said: "I agree, they want to be included and want to be needed, but very often on their own terms. They also need to be sensitive to our needs and schedules. It is often difficult for me with my large family to give to singles the quality time they would like. That's why a successful relationship is never a one-way street. Each one of us has to give that which we would like to receive."

I found that one of the hardest things for me as a widow was to accept the fact that I no longer had anyone for whom I was number one. It took courage for me to accept my vulnerability and expose this wound. In the garden of Eden, God said to Adam, "It is not good for man [woman] to be alone." He created within us the need to belong.

That hole is still in my heart. Facing it honestly has helped me to live with it. When I shared my pain with Katrine, she wisely reminded me that I must again revert to the time of adolescence and learn anew the secret of living with unfulfilled desires.

Love and the Single Woman

A single woman of middle age, disabled with a crippling disease, shared with her pastor that one of the most difficult aspects of being alone and disabled was that people did not see her as a sexual being.

Carole Streeter underlines the same thought: "Whatever our marital status, present or past, we want men to treat us as women, as creatures with the potential, at least, of being attractive. . . . We want recognition that human sexuality is much more than physical sexual encounter. We want to be sure that we are looking into our mirrors and seeing creatures who are every bit as much women as those who are married."[2]

Rebecca Pippert tells about two unmarried women who wanted romance and love. One of the women thought she should die to the idea of romantic love, while the other said, "Sex is evil—I thought when I became a Christian, my drives would go away." Rebecca told them, "You can no more cease being sexual than you can cease breathing. And who says becoming a Christian makes you dry up sexually?" She went on to explain that our yearning for sex and romance often closely parallels our yearning for God.[3]

First let's get things in focus. No stage in life is permanent. A happily married woman can become a widow in one short moment. Or a single woman can meet Mr. Right and start to plan her wedding day. The challenge we have to face is the same, whether we are married or single: to live a fulfilled life in spite of many unfulfilled desires.

My late husband in *Love Is a Feeling to Be Learned* wrote:

Love is a feeling to be learned by the single person as well. Those who do not marry do not have to give up love, but they have to learn love which gives up—just as those who are married must learn it. One could even say that the desire to be married is the condition for a happy single life. Though the task we have to face is the same, whether we are married or single, let us not make the mistake of thinking that our present state is permanent. Let us not burden our hearts with the fear of finality. Marriage can be a task for a limited time and then it suddenly ends with the death of one partner. Being single can also be but a passing task.[4]

A confident woman has to learn tough love when she is at the beginning of what may become a love relationship. Here are some suggestions I have found helpful and that may help you recognize the person God wants you to marry.

• Don't think about getting married until you are grown up. It's good for the young woman to be at least twenty-three or twenty-four years old—old enough to know who she is and to have learned how to live alone. It often takes a young man longer than that.

- Look carefully at your friend's parents. Child abusers create child abusers. How does his father treat his mother? Wife abuse is also handed down from father to son. How long has your beloved been a Christian? What kind of grandparents does he have?

- Don't let the relationship move too fast in its infancy. Take it one step at a time.

- Respect precedes love. Get to know your friends in normal settings. Wash clothes, go shopping, clean house for an older person. Hang wallpaper. You really find out who the other person is when you do a project together.

- Watch for selfishness in your love affair. Neither the man nor the woman should do all the giving.

- Don't be blind to warning signs that tell you that your potential partner is basically disloyal, hateful, spiritually uncommitted. A bad marriage is far worse than the most lonely state of being single.

- Don't marry the person you think you can live with; marry only the individual you think you can't live without.

- Don't even think of marriage without talking over these questions and the differences you may have in your expectations:

- Do you want to have children? How soon? How many?

- Where will you live?

- Will the wife work? How soon? How about after the children are born?

- How will you relate to your in-laws?

- How will money be spent?

- Where will you attend church?

If the differences are too great, far better that the marriage should never occur. A broken engagement is also easier to deal with than a divorce. Get some kind of counseling. Talk to your pastor or a trusted person or attend a retreat for engaged couples. Take a personality inventory to see if you really know and understand each other.

Living in Peace with Your Sexuality

I was asked to spend a weekend with a small group of deaconesses. They all had responsible positions as directing officers of large hospitals and medical centers in former East Germany. They had read our books and wanted advice not only as to how they could live in peace with their own sexuality but also how to help the student nurses and many young people who were being trained at their institutions. I was impressed by this group of confident women and their openness in tackling this difficult subject.

Their secret, I found, was that they had said yes to their femininity and at the same time had learned to value and express appropriately their more masculine gifts. Because they were balanced, whole women, they could help other single women who might be struggling with an addiction to masturbation or who wanted to be free from a lesbian relationship.

One of the best ways to live in peace with our sexuality is to be aware of our five senses: What is my favorite taste, smell, sound, sight, and touch? Feeling a brisk breeze blowing in your face, being encircled by water when you swim or take a relaxing bath, fresh cotton sheets, a gourmet meal—all can be deeply enjoyed by our senses. I gave one of my deaconess friends an elegant housecoat—different from the utilitarian bathrobe that she had been wearing. It helped her say yes to herself and her deep feeling of being a woman.

Virginia Satir, mother of family therapy, said at a workshop that I attended shortly before her death, "Every one of us has

13.5 square feet of skin, the largest organ of our bodies. It's all full of holes, aching to be touched."

I asked one of the deaconesses what she liked about her body.

"It's all hidden under these clothes," she said, for they were all wearing the habits of their motherhouses. "I would like so much for someone to hold me in their arms." When I gave her a hug, she said, "That does me a lot of good." I believe that confident women as well as men can not only give good hugs but also receive them.

An older woman who had recently become a widow was visiting me. My brother John, a doctor, greeting her, instinctively gave her a hug. She wrote me later to say how much healing she had received from that hug. "It was the first time a man had hugged me since my husband's death," she said.

Over the years Walter and I have received hundreds of deep letters from those who have asked us about masturbation. I'm not talking about a passing stage of life when it happens occasionally. I mean when it has become an addiction, both for single and married people. One of our books, *My Beautiful Feeling,* is a correspondence with a sincere young Christian woman who wanted to be free from this addiction. We explained to her that our sexuality is given to us as a means of expression, of communion with another person. When, as in the case of masturbation, the giver and the receiver of this expression become the same person, a quandary develops. It's like a short circuit.

More often than not, masturbation is a symptom of loneliness, of being misunderstood, a longing for love, which if satisfied in this way, does not really satisfy but leaves a greater emptiness than ever. Invariably there is a feeling of self-hatred instead of a feeling of healthy self-respect.

We received a letter from Elsie, a young woman who was masturbating to console herself when she was troubled. She asked for help in getting out of the habit. Walter wrote, "In such a situation you must make a little speech to yourself and say, 'Elsie, listen! You are discouraged now and need comfort. But masturbation is not real consolation. Afterwards you will feel more desperate and more lonesome than before and therefore long for more consolation. So it's better not to give in. Otherwise you'll get into a vicious circle.'"

Living in peace with our sexuality has a good deal to do with our self-respect. "The single life is not incompatible with happiness," Father John Catoir writes.

God made us for happiness, an eternity of it. . . . Sometimes keeping your self-respect in the process is the greatest challenge of all. Here are some ideas for growth in self-respect:

Choose your friends wisely. We are known by the friends we keep.

Select stimulating, rewarding and meaningful activities.

Find someone in real need, an elderly person, a handicapped child, someone who is sickly or alone. Get involved in making that one person a little happier.

Enjoy the Lord. Let your faith be alive to the reality of God's Unchanging Love. Receive the blessings of love and mercy which He has for you each day.

The single person needs support, a network of emotional and personal relationships. It is not easy, but neither is a commitment to a successful marriage.[5]

When the Single Life Is Not Your Choice

Some women have not chosen the single life but because of divorce and widowhood are alone. Many of them are single parents. In biblical times this group had an extended family to fall back on, and with arranged marriages, the unmarried didn't stay single very long. In our culture today it's a different story. Nearly one child in four lives with just one parent.

Carole Streeter writes:

Singleness is a resource to be used, a way of life with certain possibilities that I would not have if I were married. Part of being adult is to accept what I have and to use it as fully as I can.

God does have a mirror in which we can see the only accurate reflection of who we are. But we will never see it as long as we carry in our minds what we have determined must be a part of our lives. . . .

> . . . What I am to be is seen by love alone.
> For only love can find the way
> past this day's limitations,
> confidently grasp the sureness of tomorrow.[6]

My entrance into the single life was not voluntary. It happened with the sudden death of my husband more than a decade ago. I asked myself, Have I accepted being alone, even embraced it as God's will for this time of my life, so that I can draw out all the gifts and possibilities from this deep well that God has entrusted to me in my single life?

I asked my friends who are in this state, "What has helped you in being a single parent and in mastering the single life?" We boiled down their answers to the five *F's: Faith, Fortitude, Friends, Fellowship, Focus.*

A Case for Chastity

If you have chosen the single life, or even if you are unwillingly single because of abandonment, divorce, or widowhood, I would like to present a case for chastity. It is possible to live a full and complete life without the expression of genital sexuality but certainly not without love and affirmation.

When we talk about chastity to anyone who is not married, and I'm thinking especially of teenagers, we need to tell them that their destiny is controlled not by their sex organs but by their minds. Chastity is not prudishness. It is an attitude, an inner strength. Chastity is a spiritual energy that helps to break the bonds of selfishness.

Chastity is a decision to be free. It is the freedom from the pressures of sex, the fear of pregnancy, the devastation of diseases, quick weddings and fatherless children, guilt and pain, and hazards of birth control and the loss of personal choice.

Dietrich Bonhoeffer, a great German Christian who was killed during World War II in prison a few days before the liberation, once said that the essence of chastity is not the suppression of lust but the total orientation of one's life toward a goal.[7]

In his book *God Is a Matchmaker*, Derek Prince, former Cambridge professor, writes:

> Celibacy is like damming a river—if the river of sex is dammed, a correspondingly greater volume of spiritual, intellectual and emotional energy may be released to other forms of expression—such as intercession, scholarship, artistic creativity, or service to the poor.
>
> Surrender of the sex drive breaks its tyranny and power. . . . People who do the greatest work in the world are strongly-sexed people who subordinate sex to the ends for which they live. Remember the strongly-sexed can strongly serve."[8]

One of the greatest roots of confidence is the ability to live chaste lives, out of which we develop self-respect and mutual respect. We learn to be responsible in love, which means absolute chastity before marriage and absolute fidelity in marriage.

Jesus remained single. Many people whom I greatly respect and desire to emulate have been zealous, unrestricted Christian singles. They know the secret of living a full and complete life, even though celibate.

In a seminar on spirituality, Father Basil Pennington told us, "When I felt the call to be single, and knew that I would have to give up something as good as marriage to be a monk, then I determined that I was going to be the very best monk possible."

At the end of one of our Quiet Waters retreats, we invited each couple to sit in two chairs in the midst of our circle, and then we prayed for them and blessed them. But there were also some singles present. The leader invited one of the single women to take her place and left the empty chair at her side. "We are all married," he said. "There's just the difference between the 'two-person couples' and the 'one-person couples.' Jesus left his father for you on Christmas Day. He left his mother for you on Good Friday. He cleaves to you as a husband to his wife, no matter how difficult it is to live with you. Jesus wants to become one with you in Holy Communion."

❀ 7 ❀

Confident in Marriage

When I was in my twenties, I worked as a missionary teacher for almost two years in French Cameroon. Once a week we received our mailbag at the station. Only one item in it was of paramount interest to me, and that was a little blue aerogram sent from a young vicar serving in a five-thousand-member parish in Ludwigshafen, Germany. He had asked me to marry him, and on October 15, 1951, we had celebrated our engagement—a continent apart. I remember walking in the orange grove at the station that evening. It was a romantic setting, the light of the moon in the African night and the fragrance of the orange blossoms. But my heart rebelled. Is this the way to get engaged? I thought. We had even agreed to keep it secret, since we had no idea when we could set our wedding date.

Finally the time of waiting came to an end. At a special meeting of our missionary community when they came to pick up their children for Christmas vacation, I told my co-workers of my engagement, and they voted that I have a leave of absence at the end of the school year. My sister had sent me a pattern, some satin and embossed organdy, and I had spent happy hours every Saturday afternoon fashioning and sewing my wedding dress. We had no electricity, so I did it by turning the hand crank on my little portable sewing machine. When it was finished I modeled it for my students. (Twenty-five years later, my eldest daughter wore that same wedding dress in Cambridge, Massachusetts.)

The last day of school finally arrived. My suitcases were packed and put in a pickup for the long day's travel to Ngaoundéré, where I was to get a flight to Fort-Lamy, Chad, and from there an overnight flight to Paris. I went through a kind of culture shock as I boarded the Air France plane and realized that I was no longer surrounded by friendly African faces. I was entering that cold, somewhat distancing "white" world. I shivered a little as I took my place in the elegant plane.

Where was this great feeling of elation, even confidence, that I had assumed I would have once I got this far? I couldn't sleep as we crossed over the Sahara that night. I thought of the words of Theo Bovet, the pioneer Christian marriage counselor in Europe: "First you choose the one you love, and then you love the one you have chosen." I couldn't feel much, but I knew I was going in the right direction.

Two days later I was seated in the second-class compartment on the day train from Paris to Kaiserslautern, Germany. When I got off this train, I would meet a man I hadn't seen for two years, a man who spoke a different language than I did, who had a different heritage. He had fought on one side in World War II and my two older brothers had been on the other side. The scars of the war were still evident when I looked out the train window.

It was May 15, 1952, and in two weeks we were to be married in Mannheim. I had a sealed blue envelope in my purse, nestled safely against my passport. On the outside of the envelope were written these words: "Not to be opened until you are in the train."

I was all alone in my compartment as I took out the letter, written in German in Walter's bold, even script, and began to read:

Dear Ingrid,

This is one of the greatest hours of your life.

In a few hours you will be encountering a person in a way that you have never yet encountered a person. You will meet that person with whom you will share your life. What he is and how he is—that will be decisive for your whole life. That is the uniqueness of this encounter.

The person you will meet is a person—not a god. He has many faults and weaknesses and is in constant battle with himself. He does not want to be idolized by you. He only wants to be as he is—and as he is, he wants to be loved by you.

The person that you will be meeting is a man. That means, that at least in the beginning he will hide his deepest feelings, because he believes that it is unmanly to reveal them. At the same time, his heart is overcome by the greatness of this moment. That's why he will act as if it's something that happens every day. In the first minutes of the encounter he will probably flee into conversation about the practical things close at hand, and he will be happy that they are there. He will try to hide his deep inner feelings and will be proud of himself if he succeeds. That's how foolish a man is. That is why you shouldn't be fooled by him. How he really is—that's up to you to perceive and to ascertain.

But he will not always be like this. He just wants to bridge over those first moments of embarrassment, and take you to a lonely place where he has you all to himself and where he can reveal his true feelings to you.

He has never opened up to another person as he has opened up to you. That is why he is also trembling as he thinks of the encounter with you. For he knows that you shall be that person whom he will allow to see through him, just as he allows God to see through him. In the trembling though, there is a holy joy—joy that such a person exists.

He loves you. He has made up his mind to say yes to you as you are. It is easy for him to say this yes, because he knows that he can say it to no other person.

He loves you. He is ready to give himself up to you and knows that he will come out of the encounter a different man than he was before. He does not want to be changed by anyone else, but from you he expects it. He is not ashamed in front of you.

He loves you. He wants to be able to give you all that he has. God has given him many things. He is very happy when he can also give it to you. For himself alone he doesn't want to have anything. With his ministry, his service for others and his work, he would like to conquer your heart.

The train will only stop a few more times and then he will stand before you. You must be very calm and composed. The greatest hours of God in our lives are the more powerful if we keep a calm and quiet heart.

Yours,

Walter

Maybe it's only now, forty years later, that I have begun to understand what Walter wanted to tell me in his train letter. There was little of romance but much of love in the letter. I'm still dipping out of the reservoir of that love, which goes beyond the grave and is a mirror of Christ's love.

I learned that although love includes romance, it is not exclusively that. In a poem Marjorie Holmes expressed the difference between romance and love:

Romance is flying.
    Love is safe landing.

Romance is seeking perfection.
    Love is forgiving faults.

Romance is fleeting.
> Love is long.

Romance is the anguish of waiting for the phone to ring to
bring you words of endearment.
> Love is the anguish of waiting for a call that will
> assure you that someone else is happy and safe.

Romance is eager—striving always to appear attractive to each
other.
> Love is two people who find beauty in each other—no
> matter how they look.

Romance is dancing in the moonlight, gazing deep into
desired eyes across a candlelit table.
> Love says, "You're tired, honey. I'll get up this time,"
> as you stumble through the darkness to warm a
> bottle
> or comfort a frightened child.

Romance is flattering attention.
> Love is genuine thoughtfulness.

Romance is suspense, anticipation, surprise.
> Love is dependability.

Romance is tingling excitement.
> Love is tenderness, constancy, being cherished.

Romance is delicious.
> Love nourishes.

Romance can't last.
> Love can't help it.[1]

Helping a Man Grieve

In his letter Walter wrote about how he as a man would try to cover up his feelings. He did not want to appear "unmanly" when we met again after a separation of two years. He succeeded very well in pretending that he was the master of his heart. His mother had told me of his deep sensitivity and compassion, which she considered unique gifts for his work as a pastor and counselor. Yet I must admit in the first years of our marriage, I often had a difficult time recognizing these traits in him.

One of my secret prayers during the twenty-seven years that I was the wife of Walter Trobisch was that one day I might see tears in his eyes. He had explained to me that since his experiences as an eighteen-year-old infantryman in Hitler's army in the battle of Stalingrad, he had never been able to weep. Although he had a happy childhood, he was taught as a youth that men do not show their feelings. Then came the war—too terrible to imagine—and finally he studied theology, where again there was no place for feeling one's feelings.

My prayer was answered. After we were married almost a decade we were separated for six weeks. Cameroon was in the process of becoming independent, and Cameroon Christian College, where we were teaching, was in a dangerous fighting zone. I was expecting a baby, and for delivery I had to fly to our mission hospital fifteen hundred miles inland, where the political situation was peaceful. When Walter received the telegram telling of the safe arrival of our third son, Stephen Walter, he told me that his eyes filled with tears of joy and relief. Later I was to see his tears myself: tears of grief over sin, tears of concern for the choices our soon-to-be-adult children were making. We both learned to see the hurt behind the emotions we felt, and it gave our marriage a new dimension.

"We need someone to understand us in our weakness," Walter wrote in his prologue to *The Misunderstood Man.* "Despite the women's and men's movement it is still hard for men to grieve or talk about their fears. They suffer silently. Even in Africa, men are trying to get this message across. The owner of a minibus in Accra, Ghana, had this sign printed on the side of his bus, 'Man is suffering, but woman don't know it.'[2]

A pastor told of the loss of his beloved father from a sudden heart attack. A year later his grandfather died. Good memories of them both overwhelmed him, but he locked up his feelings in an armor of stoicism. Shortly after that, he and his family went to serve for a time in Kenya. His African helper, N'galu, informed him that an old man in one of the families they had visited together had died. So the two men, one black and one white, went to the funeral.

When they arrived in the village, the relatives of the deceased, even his sons, were crying. They poured out their grief in loud wails, while the women sang and did the mourning dance, shaking their dry gourds filled with corn.

As the missionary and N'galu drove home, they were silent. The pastor who had shut up his own grief was haunted by the sound of those sons weeping for their father. When they reached home, they stood together looking toward Mount Kilimanjaro. N'galu put his hand on the white man's shoulder and said, "It is good to cry for our fathers and our grandfathers. Tears wash the pain out of our hearts."

Something gave way inside the pastor. He sat down on the steps and began to cry for his own father and grandfather. At last he'd found time to weep. When he returned to the States a year later, he was not the same man. He'd learned to cry his tears and not hide his feelings.

I'm convinced that men do not hide their feelings from women. When they look in their hearts, they simply don't see anything there. As the author Robert Bly explains, "This feeling of numbness comes on early in life. Grief is the door to that feeling."[3]

Alice Miller, the Swiss psychologist, writes, "When you were young, you needed something you did not receive, and you will never receive it. Mourning is the proper attitude, not blame."[4] One challenge for the confident woman is to encourage her husband to grieve for that which he did not have.

Love and True Sexuality

Before we can have the right relationship with men, we must understand what true sexuality is and also feel at home with our own sexuality.

When Mrs. Stanley Baldwin, wife of a post-Victorian prime minister, prepared her daughters for marriage, she suggested that they close their eyes and think of England as the best way to endure sexual intercourse. A decent, godly woman didn't have a desire for sexual intercourse. It was a part of the fallenness of male nature and, regrettably, the only way to have babies. The assumption that sexual passion is a result of the Fall rather than the good idea of the Creator probably goes back to Augustine in the fourth century.

"Celebrate your sexuality" is what I would like to tell women and men. God made us body-persons. The Bible begins with the body, in creation, and it ends with the body, in resurrection. God didn't make a soul and then wrap a body around it. The soul does not drive the body around like an angel driving an automobile. The biblical story is not about the creation of a soul that is encumbered by a body; it is about a body that comes alive to God.

In Gen. 1:27 we read, "God created humankind in his own image, in the image of God created he him, male and female created he them." It is man and woman together who reflect God's image. Sexuality as part of God's image is what drives us toward intimacy. C. S. Lewis once said, "Sexual attraction is the essential spark that gets the engine of marriage going in the first place, even though it is a quieter steadier agapic love that fuels it for the long run."[5]

Married women need to know that as they grow older, their sexual experiences can only become richer and deeper. "Sex is a 20-year warm-up" says Charlie Shedd. If that is true, then the older a couple becomes, the more joy they can have together in sexual union. It is the confident wife who is ready to court her husband sometimes, to invite him to find the rest that only she can give him in their sexual union. Then she too will be refreshed and have the zest to cope with the myriad details that make up her life.

"God designed us to enjoy sex," say John and Paula Sanford. He united our sensitive spirits to delicately intricate, wondrously strong, feeling bodies to give us great heights of blessing and joy in sexual union. There is nothing we can do with one another through our bodies that is so holy and perfectly fulfilling as much as sexual union. God meant it for refreshment, fulfillment, recreation, realignment, release, sharing, procreation, healing, lessons in loving, practice in sensitivity, development in the art of laying down our lives for another, completion, entrance into the kingdom of being corporate, gratitude, longing, hope, endurance, fun, laughter, mysticism, embrace and so on through endless catalogues of blessing. It is perhaps God's best physical gift to mankind.[6]

Sexual intimacy is important during the middle years when often both husband and wife are dealing with stress. This is a time for couples to draw together physically, emotionally, and spiritually and to discover the true strength of couple power.

In our Quiet Waters retreats for couples and singles we talk at length about the three essentials of a marriage according to Gen. 2:24: leaving, cleaving, and becoming one flesh. When one of these three is lacking, a sick marriage will result. If there is not a good sexual relationship, there will be a hungry marriage. If there is no real cleaving, there will be an empty marriage. If there is no leaving, there will be a stolen marriage.

A Lasting Marriage

Jim and Sally Conway have written about the ten traits of a lasting marriage. In a survey of couples whose marriages had survived, these traits were described as crucial for holding marriage together:

1. A commitment to stay married and to keep their marriage as a high priority
2. Ability to communicate
3. Personal spiritual life
4. Resolving conflicts
5. Relationships with others—a circle of friends
6. Sexual intimacy
7. Sharing fun, leisure, and humor
8. Realistic expectations
9. Serving each other and sharing leadership
10. Growing personally[7]

If you were to rate your marriage on a scale of 10 percent to 100 percent, where would you score yourselves according to each of these ten traits?

I recently read the moving story of Pat and Jill Williams in their book *Rekindled*.[8] After ten years of marriage, in which Jill had to take second place to her husband's profession as manager of one of the country's best basketball teams, the marriage was dying. Jill could no longer respond to her husband, not even in words. It was as if her heart were dead. Then Pat began to court his wife and try to win her back. At first she was afraid of being hurt again, so she kept her heart in steel armor. Her love was paralyzed. Pat was not a man to give up, so he continued the four steps he had learned from Ed Wheat, physician and marriage counselor, called B-E-S-T. This is an acronym representing the four positive elements that will transform any marriage. They stand for B-blessing, E-edifying, S-sharing, and T-touching.

Blessing means good words, kind actions, thankful appreciation, and intercessory prayer for your partner.

Edifying means building up, encouraging, and affirming each other.

Sharing means giving of yourself, listening to your partner, and developing a sensitive awareness of how to deepen the love between you.

Touching tells another that she is cared for. It can calm fears, soothe pain, bring comfort, and give the blessed satisfaction of emotional security.

One day when Pat felt the first flicker of response from his wife, he called Dr. Wheat. "Why did it take me ten years to discover this? Why am I just now finding out about this?"

"Three basic reasons," Dr. Wheat said in a slow and deliberate manner. "We men are very, very slow learners, very stubborn and very selfish. Be grateful you found out. Most men never do, or if they do, it's too late."

Jill learned how to respond, and together they learned a new definition of love that Dr. Wheat had given them: "Love is the power that will produce love as I learn to give it rather than strain to attract it."

Sexual Abuse and Incest

Some women have difficulties in marriage because they were abused sexually earlier in life. It may have been by a father, a brother, an uncle, or some other trusted adult.

If you were abused either emotionally, verbally, sexually, or physically, then it is important to face this pain and to confront your abuser. Confrontation is nothing more than a sharing of facts and feelings. It will enable you to open new doors to your center, that center which Linda Leonard speaks of when she describes the way many women are cut off from a part of themselves and live in only a few of the rooms in their "mansion." Exploring the pain of the past, admitting it, and then confronting it—all this is a part of being an important person to yourself, a secret that many women still have to explore.

Estimates say that one out of every three women has been sexually abused. When a woman is raped or is the victim of incest, she feels dirty and worthless. She may feel that she is no longer her own person, that the man involved has taken away a part of her (emotionally) that can never be replaced. She may then feel that she would be unworthy, perhaps not even be able, to be a wife and a mother. She may see herself as a fresh, white garment, that has been trampled in the mud, and no matter how often that garment is washed, it will never be white and pure and beautiful again.

I have a good friend who learned how to face the pain of incest. My friend said that because of this experience with her father, she always felt on edge, wary of contact of any kind, and she kept her distance both emotionally and physically. Even though her father was an excellent provider and a good husband to her mother, this part of his nature always tended to overshadow all the good things he was and he did in the mind of his daughter.

She didn't know whether to tell her mother. She chose not to because she was afraid it would hurt her mother too much. All she could do was to leave home as soon as possible, build her own life, and hope that no one would ever know. But what she had experienced would color all her relationships with men.

She wrote to me after many years of walking intimately with her Lord:

I doubt if anyone can truly forgive and forget the hurt without God's love and assurance that they are "OK in Him."

I believe that the only way that total and *permanent* healing and happiness can come is if the woman will allow Jesus to take her by the hand and bring her to His Father and present her to God the Father as *His* daughter. When she can then see herself accepted, as she is, with all the (to her) shame and horror of the past, as a daughter of her heavenly Father, she can then be lifted out of the mire of the past to "sit with Him in heavenly places." She can say with faith and hope, My earthly father was not a good father to me, but my Father in heaven is able to be to me here on earth that Father on whom I can totally rely for now and all that is ahead.

She can say, He will daily love me and He will enable me to forgive my natural father, so that the events of the past will not spoil the future that my loving Father in heaven has planned for me. I will compare my suffering with Jesus' suffering, and see that with Him who understands suffering, I can keep going. I will accept His forgiveness of all my faults and sins and in His strength and by His grace through His forgiveness, forgive my father, because my heavenly Father has forgiven me so much more.

Even if I cannot forget the past completely (for human memory is long!) I will be able through Christ's love to remember it not with horror, shame, anger and contempt, but rather with a sense of sadness that the wonderful father-daughter relationship that we could have had did not develop as it should. My father lost so much too by being wrongly motivated. This loss I hand to my heavenly Dad and I forgive my earthly dad, so that both he and I may be set free by the cleansing blood of Jesus.

❀ 8 ❀

Confident with Children

There was a wise old Chinese man who took a walk every morning in his village. People showed their veneration by bowing to him. He in turn took off his hat and bowed low only when he met a child. This upset the elders of the village. "Why do you not show us a sign of reverence?" they asked.

"I already know who you are" was his answer. "But I don't know who this child will become."

"When you see a child, you see Jesus Christ," Martin Luther once said. Jesus said, "He who receives one of these little ones in my name, receives me" (Matt. 18:5).

If You Want Respect, Give Respect

The creation of new life is God's sign to us that he has not given up on this world. He begins all over again each time a child is born. O. E. Rölvaag's *Giants in the Earth,* a powerful novel about pioneer life in America, tells about the birth of little "Peder Victorious" in a desolate settlement in the vast Dakota prairie. The pioneers were almost ready to give up, and Peder's mother, Beret, was sure she would die in childbirth. She had already told her husband how he should bury her, for she had lost her will to live. Miraculously she survived. The birth of her little son on Christmas morning turned the tide of despair and pointed the way to the future.

"Ah, that newcomer . . . weak and insignificant . . . he beguiled the heavy-hearted folk into laughing, and what can avail against folk who laugh—who dare to laugh in the face of a winter like this one? . . . That winter it was he who saved people from insanity and the grave."[1]

My first home was on the slopes of Mount Kilimanjaro in Tanzania, East Africa. There the chief of the stalwart and industrious Chagga tribe would call his men together and say, "Take good care of the pregnant woman. She is the most important person in our tribe." No wonder these women were confident and carried themselves regally. The very future of their country was within them. A child born of such a mother and surrounded by such fathers was both valued and validated. The result? Adults who are confident, full of initiative, and able to solve problems.

My husband and I were conducting a family life seminar for black South African leaders, many of them pastors. I was introduced to one of the participants, a police officer. I was told that wherever this man was stationed, order reigned without oppression. So I asked him if he could tell me his secret. His answer was simple, "If you want respect, give respect."

My heart bleeds when I see parents, teachers, and other adults who have not understood this basic rule in their relationships with children—"If you want respect, give respect." A child is not a toy but a very real person to be respected, loved, and educated.

Instilling Confidence

We have to begin early if we are to have confident children. Without confident mothers, teachers, grandparents, we won't have confident children. That's why family life education begins long before the birth of a child. As the Germans say, "If you want to bring a child up right, you have to begin twenty-five years before the child is born." Certainly the kind of family life that we have experienced ourselves will have a lot to say about how we raise our children.

Above all, what is our basic attitude about raising a child? Is the child viewed only as a nuisance, a brat, or seen only as an heir? Or is he or she a real, healthy individual to be loved and guided?

I believe one of the greatest moments in the life of a couple is the moment of conception, when together with the Creator they can call a new life into being. In order to do this, they need to know how to live in harmony with their fertility.

The child in the womb is dependent on the health of the mother. The moment of birth should be the time of a woman's greatest dignity, when she is a co-worker with God in bringing this new life into the visible world. Newborn babies need food, warmth, and security, and all three are received best at the mother's breast, where the foundation for mutual confidence and companionship is begun.

The role of the father is basic in family life, for he is the first man that a daughter knows, and he to a great extent determines her attitude toward men later in life. Parents lay the foundations for self-esteem and self-acceptance, essential for any love relationship. Children need to know that they are unique, created in the image of God.

I believe that the family table conversation can be the greatest single influence in the life of a child. One mother told me that when she plans and prepares the menu for the evening meal, she also prays about the conversation topic for that same meal. We could learn from a videotape of our evening meal made by a hidden camera. Sometimes whiny and complaining children need to hear how they sound to others. Mothers might say with surprise, "I didn't know my voice was that shrill. I need to work on it."

Etiquette is another tool of family education. Good manners remind children that others are important. As one mother told her children, "Manners are always motivated by thoughtfulness to others, a reminder that we are not the center of the universe." Good manners are caught as well as taught. Children gain confidence when they know how to act in a given situation, for example, when they are introduced to strangers.

Raising small children is quite impossible without a certain order of mealtime, play, and sleep. Later they must learn to follow school and work schedules. In our home we did not begin a meal until all the family members were present and the table blessing had been said. No one left the table until they were excused. I like the Scandanavian practice of each child going to the mother after the meal and thanking her for the food she has prepared before asking to be excused. An easy schedule of table chores should be enforced.

"What you are speaks so loud I can't hear what you say" is certainly never more true than when raising our children. Susan and John Yates, parents of five, say in their new book *What Really Matters at Home*, "Modeling the right character qualities in your home is a constant process. As parents, we must have a deep hunger within ourselves to grow in personal integrity before God. Our children will pick up on this hunger—and as we strive to please God in our homes, our children will learn that pleasing him is the most important thing of all."[2]

I'm convinced that confident children will have so much fun exploring what is right, that wrong values will be of little interest to them. Freedom brings great responsibility. All of our skills in training will have little effect if our children are not motivated to follow that training.

George MacDonald, that great Scottish Christian and novelist of the past century, had a harmonious marriage and family life. Guests in their home were amazed at the love and respect between parents and children. MacDonald, whose writings greatly influenced C. S. Lewis, once wrote: "Let us educate our children, not so that they will do good—but so that it is impossible for them to do evil."[3]

Growing Up in Love's Overflow

Parent effectiveness is closely connected with partner effectiveness. I have often told fathers, "If you want to love your child, love the child's mother." The same goes for mothers, "If you want to love your child, love the child's father."

Joseph Bayly said it well in his little poem entitled "A Psalm of Love."

> Thank you for children
> brought into being
> because we loved.
>
> God of love,
> keep us loving
> so that they
> may grow up whole
> in love's overflow.[4]

What about the single mother, the one whose husband had left her, through divorce or death, or one who has never been married? In Genesis 16 we read the story of Hagar, who is unmarried and pregnant. She will bear Abraham's son and is in a seemingly hopeless situation. She has run away into the desert because of the quarrel with her mistress, Sara. In a miraculous way God provides a well when she is dying of thirst. The name of the well is Beer-lahairoi, which means "well to the Living One who sees me." Hagar is told by the angel of the Lord to go back to her mistress and that she will bear a son, Ishmael, whose name means "God hears."

Later, when Ishmael is a teenager, he is disrespectful to Sara and her child Isaac. This time Abraham intervenes and sends them away. They are once more in the desert facing death. When their supply of water runs out, God provides for them, and he makes of Ishmael's descendants a great nation. Hagar's story is an encouragement for those single mothers who feel they are in desperate and hopeless situations. There is a Living One who sees them and says, "If anyone is thirsty, let (her) come to me and drink" (John 37b).

Even if the physical father is absent, a child needs to have a father figure—an uncle, grandfather, youth worker, cousin, neighbor. In some of the minority neighborhoods of New York, where there are many single mothers, it was observed that the boys who began school well in the first, second, and even third grades became increasingly difficult to teach as they got older. They seemed to lose respect for their women teachers. When a group of black males came into the school as volunteer mentors and substitute fathers, there was a remarkable improvement among the boys, who up until then often had no male authority in their lives and who were in real danger of becoming women haters.

Children can know who they are only by being with people who know them well and who can give them useful information about themselves. Parents alone aren't enough to give this to their children. An African proverb says, "It takes a whole village to bring up one child." Every youth needs at least one adult mentor who believes in him or her, especially when the father is absent.

A Place for Each Child

Even in a large family, where several children share the same room, it is possible to give each child his shelf, his drawer, his box. This private space should then be respected by all family members. A basic rule for small children is "I have to know what is mine before I can know what is thine." This means teaching respect for each other's ownership and having rules for sharing.

At a women's retreat I asked the participants what the word *place* brought to their minds. Here are some of their answers: comfort, peace, sanctuary, warmth, open door, people enclosed by a moat, every animal with its own turf, placemats, storage, a comfortable chair, candles, cushions, doilies, quiet rest. Are we able to help our children create a place in which they feel safe? Only then can we dare to send them out into a cold world. Only then will they have the confidence to create places where others feel safe.

Sometimes I am called to be just an umbrella so that I can give a child, a friend, a spouse shelter from the rain. Or if I am in a tropical climate, I need to protect them from too much sun. Sometimes I am called to be a warm room, where children both large and small can come in from the cold and be fed and strengthened for the battles ahead. As one husband told his wife, "When I come home from a hard day at work, I need a place where there's no cold wind blowing." And where there are little ones, I need to make a warm nest.

I can do this only when I am in a safe place. In Ps. 27:5 we read: "In the day of trouble he will keep me safe in his dwelling; he will hide me in the shelter of his tabernacle and set me high upon a rock."

Building Trust

Basic trust originates early in life, basic trust that enables children to face the storms of life. When this basic trust is violated, the children's hearts become like sieves, and they cannot grasp the truth that they are loved.

One couple adopted a very troubled little girl. They said, "We just loved her till she felt safe. She was all closed off when she came to us. A part of Tella has not yet come home."

A friend, a professional gardener, has this motto in her home: "As the gardener, so the garden." Planting seeds, bulbs, plants, trees is one of the great joys God has entrusted to us to make his world beautiful. But what about the seeds we plant in our children's lives? What about the little trees we plant?

As mothers we must give birth to our children many times over in their lifetime. Parenting is for life, and it seems that one of our children or grandchildren will always keep us on our knees. It helped me greatly as a single mother to know that in the last instance, the problems my child may be going through are not my problems. They are God's problems. It is a constant exercise of faith for me to relinquish my children into God's hands. He is a loving Father, who loves them more deeply than I ever could.

Giving Children a History

A wise father told us how his sons would make life miserable for Mary Ellen, their seven-year-old little sister. They especially liked to tease her when the family was gathered for their evening meal. Mike, the father, said to them: "Look at Great-grandmother Mary Ellen. Someday that's what she'll be. Would you treat your great-grandmother this way?" It made the boys gasp, for they knew and respected their great-grandmother.

Giving our children a sense of time and history is a real challenge. My grandson Charles, who was five at the time, asked me one day, "Ingma, are you a blue or a gray?" He wanted to know on which side my allegiance was in the Civil War. His father had been reading a history of the War of Secession to him. I had to tell him that I was neither a blue nor a gray, that my great-grandfathers were still in Sweden at that time. One of them was very tall and was a part of the King's guard. That seemed to satisfy him.

We children never tired when our parents would tell us how our great-grandparents had come across the Atlantic in sailing vessels. Cholera had broken out on the ship, and several of the passengers died. One of them was a little boy, eighteen months old. His name was Peter Andrew, and his father, Daniel, was my great-grandfather. My great-grandmother, Anna, could not bear to be present as her little boy's body was lowered into the ocean, so her husband and daughter Sophia had to stand by. Later Daniel and Anna had another son, who was born in their new country. His name was Henry Edward, and he was my grandfather.

I keep Henry's picture in my library. He was a businessman and helped run a hardware store in the frontier town of Kearney, Nebraska, before he became a farmer himself. I visited Bethany Church in Axtell, where the family worshiped a hundred years ago and where Henry was an elder. I also found out that Henry and Tillie, my grandmother, team-taught a Sunday school class at Bethany.

I fell in love with that grandfather whom I never knew. Henry died tragically, the result of a fall from a wagon pulled by runaway horses, after he had sold a load of wheat for missions.

My aunt described my grandfather: "He was a man of discipline—a man of order and care. But he was also loving and tender. Whenever one of us had a birthday, we had a special treat in store. The birthday child would climb into Father's comfortable lap during morning devotions. There was no better place. At Christmas he was a child with us."

We find out who we are by knowing where we came from. My own confidence is strengthened when I think of my grandfather and imagine what a safe place his lap would have been.

A mother in Tanzania was putting her baby to sleep by singing to her the list of her ancestors. With each pat on the baby's bottom, the mother gave the name of one of the baby's forefathers and foremothers. Then this African mother decided that Baby Jesus should have his own lullaby, so she made up a song for him using the genealogy of the Old Testament. Here's the refrain of the song:

> Hush, little Jesus boy, Alleluia,
> Dry your tears, Jesus boy, Alleluia.
> Sweet child of Mary, Alleluia
> Treasure of Joseph, Alleluia

With my own children I found it helpful to treat each child as an only child at least once a week. We would go for a walk together, go shopping, do some artwork, play a game, or read aloud. There will be quality time only if we also have quantity time with our children.

Swim, Dive, and Dance

Walter often said that every girl should learn to swim, dive, and dance in order to be at home with her body and to prepare for a happy marriage. A wife must be able to give herself to her husband. Her love and confidence in him make her able to abandon all her fears. She lets go of herself like a bird flying in the air or a fish swimming in the sea. But to do this she must like herself and feel a deep satisfaction in being a woman.

I remember watching our children learning how to dive. For the boys it did not seem difficult to mount the high diving board, take a light jump, and then spring into the deep water below. When they had done it once, they were eager to try it over and over again. But for our eldest daughter, it was different. Each time she mounted the diving board, instead of running and jumping off it like her brothers did, she hesitated and then in fear drew back. Her brothers kept encouraging her and urging her to try it, but it was only when her father dived ahead of her and was ready to receive her in the water that she was daring enough to do it, discovering in this way a new joy in her young life.

In Austria, where our children had their education, it was customary for young people to learn ballroom dancing at the age of sixteen. Since this was not included in my education, I took a course in dancing after I was forty, just so we could have this joy as a family. Even at our marriage retreats, when things got too serious, we learned that inserting a waltz, a polka, or a folk dance brought new vitality and joy into couples' relationships.

Swimming, diving, dancing—these are good images of what the confident wife experiences in the act of love. She dives into the deep water, but she is not afraid, because she knows that her loving husband is there waiting to receive her with open arms.

Certainly one of the most essential steps in preparing our daughters to be confident women—and competent wives—is to teach them about their own bodies. Instead of so-called sex education, I prefer the term *fertility self-awareness*. Fertility is the power we have to give life to another human being.

Fertility appreciation is based on fertility self-awareness, which goes beyond body parts and functions. We need to give our daughters (and sons) knowledge as the key to fertility appreciation. Knowledge is the first step to appreciation of music, art, history, nature, another person, or even ourselves.

We need to teach them that the primary sex organ for both the male and female is the brain. The brain controls the male and female physical aspects of sexuality. It is also in the brain that perceptions, decisions, and choices about the use of our sexual powers are made. It is the boss of both the male and female reproductive system. We need to teach that the tremendous power of fertility also carries with it a big responsibility. Just as with learning to drive, it's not enough to learn how to put the key in the ignition, one must learn the proper places to drive, how to use the brakes, follow the traffic laws. It's vital to learn how to control the power one has in order to avoid harming oneself or others.[5]

"Have Them, Love Them, Let Them Go"

It was Robert Bradley, author of *Husband-Coached Childbirth,* who used this phrase to consolidate his message on child rearing. I found the last one the most difficult—to let my children go. To watch my eldest daughter march off to school was a heartbreaking experience, and I'm not sure it was any easier when she was eighteen and left home in Austria to go to college in the States. But without the leaving, there will no returning— no real coming home. For a mother, this leaving begins with the cutting of the umbilical cord. Mothers remember the strange emptiness of the womb as the warmth of that little person leaves. Both mother and child must learn to be independent.

Walter wrote down these journal entries for me when he visited Katrine at Garoua-Boualai, where there was a school for the children of missionaries in central Cameroon. I had taught at this school myself the year before I was married. It had a good atmosphere, and the houseparents were very special people and our good friends. We entrusted our child to them. This is what he wrote:

Midday siesta. Outside a hot wind blows across the steppes. Cooking and boiling, the wind sounds exactly like a burning fire in a tile stove on a winter day. The cool atmosphere of this room breathes the same shelteredness as a heated room does on a cold day.

As I awake I am not alone. In the next bed my child's fresh and short breathing flows deep and regularly. The way she is sleeping makes me feel good. She is living and growing. In comparison to the sound of the deadening wind, her breathing is as clear as a fresh, bubbling spring.

She raises her head, sees me, smiles, and falls back into the pillow again. She repeats this several times, but then she gets out of bed. She smiles and says nothing. There are only two expressions on her face: the seriousness of being absorbed when she is making her bed, eating, doing her homework— and this smile.

She looks at the page I've written. She studies it. Then she smiles as if she wants to participate, to understand a part of me. She picks up a pencil and in deep concentration begins to draw hearts, many hearts. The dark golden hair, which she is letting grow so that she can have braids, falls forward and almost covers her face.

The child cries. The ugly wart on her heel has to be removed. She complains softly, but her hand rests firmly in mine as we walk together to the mission hospital. Her confidence is greater than her fear.

She refuses to lie down on the operating table. Her head cuddled on my chest, she sits up without flinching and observes the doctor's hand: the inserting of the needle for the local anesthesia—five or six times—the cutting of the scalpel, the sewing up of the incision. The unknown has given way to the known. There are no more tears. From her place of shelteredness she looks out onto that which is hostile and foreign. We are completely one and belong together. As we go back, she strides like a heroine, victoriously joyful.

This is life: this togetherness in quietness and joy with nothing happening, at least nothing you can put your finger on. Why do we think such times don't count? Why do we really live only on the days we steal from our work?

"I don't care if you go now. You've been here long enough," she tells me on the evening of the third day. This belonging together and yet independent—how wonderful!

A Word About Teenagers

Often our teenagers have what David Elkind calls a "patchwork sense of self." We assume the teenager is a kind of adult. They are not adults and they are not children; they are "unplaced." If they are to grow up to be confident persons, they need a protected period of time to find out who they are. Only with this secure sense of self will the young person be able to deal with both the inner and outer demands of life.

I often tell parents to think about wrapping their teenagers in a cocoon of cotton wool. Into this cocoon they pour love and more love. No picking at them. Just keep pouring that love into them. One fine day the cocoon will burst open and out of it will emerge this wonderful human being.

A teenager who was having trouble with his parents told them one day at the table, "If we couldn't all laugh together around this table, I wouldn't be able to stand this family." We had a little picture in our dining room with these words on it, "Love and laughter hold us together."

The Joy of Grandparenting

"Becoming a grandparent is a stage of life there's nothing wrong with," a friend said recently. I can only agree. Seven grandsons have been born to me since Walter's death, and I have three granddaughters. Knowing that I am not responsible for their twenty-four-hours-a-day care, week in and week out, I can enjoy those special times when they visit me or when I am a visitor in their parents' homes. I even have a number of "adopted" grandchildren, giving me a unique chance to show these children too that I am in love with them. In order to prosper, a child needs an adult who believes in her completely and who is on her side. This is the privilege of grandparents.

Walter often told me about his doting German grandparents, with whom he spent several weeks each summer. Their love did not spoil him; it helped give him a sense of his own worth and a knowledge of his roots.

My grandmother became my role model as I lived with her my first two years of high school. She personified for me the confident woman described in Prov. 31:25, 26: "She is clothed with strength and dignity; she can laugh at the days to come. She speaks with wisdom, and faithful instruction is on her tongue."

There was a hidden strength about her that reminded me of Swedish steel, which stands up under great pressure because of the quality of the ore used to produce it. Through her life and death I learned some of these secrets. She, just like my mother, was widowed at the age of forty-three, left with a large family to raise alone.

One of the last days of her life, my grandmother called me to her bedside. My sisters and I had come to sing for her, and she had requested the song "Under His Wings, I Am Safely Abiding." Then she asked me, Ingrid, you want to go to the Sudan, don't you? You feel that this is your calling to carry on there where your father did pioneer work—but where he could not stay?" I assured her that this was my wish. "Then may I bless you to this end," she said and laid her hands upon me.

I was with her when she died in her home, her children and grandchildren at her bedside. It was the first time I had seen a loved one departing from this life. There was a gasp for air and then a look of great peace came over her face. No wonder the words of Ps. 103:17 became a firm promise for me: "The steadfast love of the Lord is from everlasting to everlasting upon those who fear him and his righteousness to children's children." I know that I am the recipient of his blessing and love, not only because I reached out in faith to receive it but because my parents and grandparents blessed me even before I was born.

I'm happy that my children also got to know their father's mother. We called her Mutti. Although she had never been out of her home country, she was courageous enough to accept our invitation to come and live with us in Africa after her husband died suddenly in Leipzig. She had to close the door behind her, knowing that she could never return because of the Iron Curtain. For three years she taught German in French to African students from thirty different tribes and worked side by side with her son, Walter, at Cameroon Christian College. It was the crowning work of her life.

At the same time she gave our children a sense of their uniqueness and value. She taught me to recognize all of the possibilities of development in a young child. "Look at your son," she said. "He's a year and a half—like a bud opening up. Every day is exciting as you observe him and his new discoveries."

When Mutti was in her seventies, she became ill with a fatal heart disease. For several months before her death we took care of her in our little Austrian home. It was a task of love, around the clock. Walter wrote at this time:

"When someone is dying, everything else takes second place," a friend said to us as we took turns watching at the bedside of my mother. This was a releasing word. Didn't we do the same thing when our children were born? Do we give death a lesser place? When we stopped trying to do our normal work in addition to nursing my mother, we became more relaxed and free.

We will never forget the hour spent with the children at their grandmother's deathbed. They asked many questions which were not easy to answer: "Where is she now?" "Can she see us?" "Will we see her again?" Afterwards we heard five-year-old Ruth say to seven-year-old Stephen, "I want to die too; then I can be with Jesus!" Later she told her mother, "Don't worry when you get old like Mutti. I'll take care of you, like you took care of her."

Blessing the Children in Your Life

God the Father affirmed his Son when he said after Jesus' baptism, "You are my Son, whom I love; with you I am well pleased" (Mark 1:11, NIV). How much more do we need to affirm and encourage our children? We need to catch them doing something right and praise them for it. The schoolchild needs kindness ("I'm on your side"), encouragement ("You can do it"), and challenge ("Now do it!"). These are practical ways that we bless our children.

If parents do not see good or value in their own children, their children can do nothing. They cannot love others because they feel that they have nothing valuable to share. I remember being asked to speak, together with my eldest son, in a large German city. People were curious about this mother–son team, so in his opening remarks my son said to the audience, "I know you are wondering about the fact that we are together on this platform. May I just say at the beginning, if a mother doesn't believe in her son, who will?"

Another way to bless a child is to follow Jesus' example: "Little children were brought to Jesus for him to place his hands on them and pray for them. . . . Jesus said, 'Let the little children come to me, and do not hinder them, for the kingdom of heaven belongs to such as these'" (Matt. 19:13–14, NIV). We can bless our children each evening as we put them to bed. Every child goes through disturbing behavior patterns. Every child has bad dreams. Pray with children, and pray for them. In our travels Walter and I were often asked by troubled parents to go to the bedside of their sleeping child and bless them.

Children can also be taught to bless their siblings. In his book on prayer, Richard Foster relates an experience that shows how easy it is for children to grasp the meaning of healing prayer.

> I was once called to a home to pray for a seriously ill baby. Her four-year-old brother was in the room and so I told him I needed his help in praying for his baby sister. He was delighted

to help and so was I, for I know that children can often pray with unusual effectiveness. He climbed up into the chair beside me. "Let's play a little game," I suggested. "Since we know that Jesus is always with us, let's suppose that he is sitting over in that chair across from us. He is waiting patiently for us to focus our attention on him. When we see him and the love in his eyes, we start thinking more about his love than about how sick Julie is. He smiles, gets up, and comes over to us. When that happens, we both put our hands on Julie, and as we do, Jesus puts his hands right on top of ours. He releases his healing light right into your little sister sort of like a whole bunch of soldiers who go in and fight the bad germs until they are all gone. Okay?" Seriously the boy nodded. Together we prayed just as I had described it to him and then we thanked God that this was the way it was going to be. Amen. While we prayed, I sensed that my small prayer partner had exercised unusual faith.

The next morning Julie was perfectly well. Now, I cannot prove to you that our little prayer game made Julie well. All I know is that Julie was healed, and that was all I needed to know.[6]

I am separated from my own children and their families, and we can be together only on special occasions. But I have their pictures. In the morning I can pick up a picture, hold that child in my heart, and commit her or him and that day to the Lord before I go about my daily work. The greatest blessing I can give them is to reassure them that they are greatly loved. It is in their homes now that I hear our family prayer,

> The steadfast love of the Lord never ceases,
>> his mercies never come to an end;
> they are new every morning;
>> great is thy faithfulness.
>
>   (Lam 3:22, 23, RSV)

III

Confident in Inner Strength

❀

❊ 9 ❊

Hidden Strength in Suffering

"You can only dig the wells of joy with the spade of suffering," I heard on a radio program. *Don't Waste Your Illness* is the title of a book by Vernon Bittner. Edith Schaeffer wrote a similar admonition, "Don't abort your afflictions."[1] In other words, learn to live with the pain until its work is done.

Physical Suffering

British actress Jill Ireland fought a courageous five-year battle against breast cancer, bringing hope and inspiration to both the ailing and the healthy. In her writing and lecturing, she spoke about her battle with the disease but even more eloquently about her self-respect and optimism in the face of a devastating illness. She called herself a survivor, not a victim. Encouraging women who had undergone mastectomies, Jill said, "Make the most of your life. . . . A breast does not make me who I am."

Michael Winner, one of her film directors, gave her this tribute: "In her final years [she died at the age of fifty-four] she transcended her fame as an actress and showed that the human spirit in adversity can be a wondrous thing. She never thought of herself and her pain. She thought of her family and her friends and of other people who suffered from cancer. It was an extraordinary spirit and in spite of the illness, the spirit never faded."[2]

For years I have lived with chronic pain in my hip. Either I can pretend it's not there, try to relieve it with painkillers, or learn to be at peace with it. Through certain exercises, weight control, and physical therapy, I can greatly reduce the pain. It can only be healed permanently, however, through surgery. That would mean an even greater pain for a while. Is it worth it?

For many years I have taught couples about the joy of childbirth—not childbirth without pain, but childbirth without fear. This can happen only when the mother knows what is happening in the birth process and can give herself up to the contractions of labor. *Travail* is the word the French use for it, which means "hard work." These contractions grow closer together and become more intense as the moment of birth approaches. With the coaching of her husband and the obstetrical team, a woman can learn to ride these waves of contractions, like riding ocean waves, or she can be overcome by them.

It's all right to feel the fear, but we mustn't stop there. Our suffering and pain need to have a purpose. John wrote in his Gospel: "A woman giving birth to a child has pain because her time has come; but when her baby is born she forgets the anguish because of her joy that a child is born into the world" (John 16:21, NIV).

Loneliness

Perhaps the greatest suffering that Jesus endured on the cross was the feeling of loneliness and abandonment. It's hard to put into words the aching of the lonely soul. I once found this definition: "Loneliness is a hole in the soul, a prisoner tapping endlessly against the stones, waiting in vain for an answering tap."

That's just how I feel when I'm lonely, isolated not by my choice, unable to make myself heard, understood, seen, accepted, valued, or loved. Physically loneliness is an acute attack of skin hunger. I ache to be held and stroked.

Loneliness is not the same as solitude. Solitude is a great gift. If I can have two hours all by myself in my study, it's like a tonic for my soul. But loneliness attacks in the dead of night. It's the bogeyman at the door. At its worst, it seems eternal—past, present, and future.

Loneliness can strike a happily married person as well as a single person. Every woman who has a hard-working husband, for example, knows loneliness. A young woman who lived for two years in our home in Austria once said to me, "There are two kinds of men I'll never marry—a doctor or a pastor. Their wives are so lonely." Of course that's true of wives of men in other professions too. Often the more professionally successful the man is, the more lonely his wife.

So what are we going to do about it? You can't always look to people, even good friends, to solve your problems. They often are not available when you think you need them. During my thirty years overseas, I often had no peers. People came from long distances to talk to Walter, but these people were looking to us for help. I had wonderful German and Austrian neighbors, but I knew they would not understand the depths of my loneliness, because they were living in their homeland while I was far from mine.

Walter was aware of my loneliness, and he listened, but he was lonely himself. As an East German, he had lost his home and his friends there after World War II. He had been a well-known youth leader in Leipzig and had many friends and relatives there, but that was behind the Iron Curtain, so he couldn't reach out to them either. Living in Austria as we did, we were both in exile.

One day in desperation I drove the thirty miles from Lichtenberg, the mountain hamlet where we lived, to Salzburg. I had seen that there was a chaplain's office at the university where people could just walk in, wait their turn, and talk over their problems. I did that and it helped. Sometimes I would write a letter to someone I thought would understand, and just the act of writing released me from my pain. The same was true about writing in my journal.

I learned to fill up those alone times. Anyone who enjoys reading never needs to stay lonely, because by reading you can get in touch with great minds and share their thoughts. Sometimes I did handwork. I have a needlepoint cushion top that went around the world with me three times before I finished it, but it helped me when I could neither read nor write. I play the piano—not very well—but I am often helped by singing or learning the words of a new hymn.

Loneliness can be a gift from God. It can be his magnet to draw us to him. He made us capable of great loneliness to ensure that we don't stagnate and that we reach beyond ourselves to him, to new experiences, and to other people, people who need us because they are lonely too.[3]

Lover's Grief

In speaking to young people as they struggled with the pain of lover's grief, Walter once said,

> Suffering is not something to be eliminated, regardless of the cost. If we live through it and accept it, suffering can become a spring of riches, of depth, growth and fulfillment—yes, of happiness.
>
> We do not learn to give up love, but we learn love which is ready to give up. Suffering can even make immature love grow into mature love. Immature, unlearned love is egotistic love. It's the kind of love that a child has—a love which claims and wants and wants immediately. It cannot endure tension and has no patience with anything which stands in the way. It demands and consumes and tries to dominate.[4]

I found a letter Walter wrote to me shortly after I reached Cameroon to begin my work there. We had just said good-bye to each other in Germany, not knowing how long our separation would be or even if God would have us together:

Dear Ingrid,

> Faith is a risk on God.
> > Life is a risk on God.
> > > Love is a risk on God.

All that we now experience will be used by the Lord in some way. Nothing will be in vain. The long darknesses we endure will become illuminating lightnings. The separation will become a finding-again, more beautiful than ever. The salt will come into our testimony through the period we now have to live through—the period of separation, of certain uncertainty, of a blind flight in a definite direction.

Let us work as if there would be no love and love as if there would be no work.

Experiencing the pain of separation and loneliness in whatever form does not weaken us but makes us stronger.

The Pain of Divorce

Those who have gone through the pain of divorce learn the same lesson. As Paula Ripple says, "Things will never be the same again. The network of relationships will never be the same. A parent will probably never experience that son- or daughter-in-law in the same way. To believe that we can rebuild or somehow reclaim what was lost is neither helpful nor true."[5]

"Most of the suffering in human life comes," says Oswald Chambers, "because we refuse to be disillusioned. For instance, if I love a human being and do not love God, I demand of that man or woman an infinite satisfaction which they cannot give. Our Lord had no illusions about men, and He knows that every relationship in life that is not based on loyalty to Him will end in disaster."

I know the pain of divorce in my own family. One of my sons came to me a few months ago to tell me that his wife had taken her clothes and computer and moved in with her parents. They had mutually agreed to file for divorce.

Speechless with shock, I knew I couldn't unload my pain as a mother on my children. Neither could I rebuild or reclaim what was lost. I had to accept the pain and try to stop the bleeding points. "In love's battles, only the wounded soldiers can serve," someone had said.

The pain became bearable only when I put it into words. In my journal I wrote a letter to my daughter-in-love. I still haven't been able to send it, and perhaps I never will. Here are some excerpts from that letter:

Dear Ann,

It's five years ago today that you graduated from college, and the next day, you and W. went to the county courthouse for your civil wedding. Before a worthy and kind judge you said your marriage vows. I was very happy as you tenderly embraced and I felt that it was right. A week later I helped you into your wedding dress and witnessed how you two said your vows again in an old church in a European city. Members of your family and friends were present. We had a wonderful wedding dinner at a cozy Italian restaurant. And then you left on your honeymoon.

Your first months of marriage were not easy, for you had to adjust to living in a small apartment in a large city, where they did not speak your language. But you were a good sport. You enrolled in language classes, learned how to shop, and often stood in line as you waited for an unfriendly clerk to serve you. You even had to carry your laundry to a laundromat several blocks away and then carry it back up the hill to dry in your little apartment. I admired how you coped with all the challenges, as you had never been out of your country before.

Now you are back in the United States. W. comes to tell me that you have left him. How did it happen? He says that you did not share the same values, or the same style of life. His dreams for the future are entirely unrealistic for you. You are hurting very much, and so your solution is to run away.

When I asked W. why he married you, he said, "Because I thought she would give me a nest in a cold and new world." He said that he feels a lot of guilt. He thinks he can pay you a generous "maintenance" sum and then you will be happy. He adds, "I will never be able to give her what she wants. I'd rather have pain now than death later on. My love for her is paralyzed."

You told me that you ran away because your husband said he didn't love you. You want him to think about money and be realistic about the future. He's so absorbed in his work that he has no time for you, so you react by getting angry and shouting at him. And the more you shout, the more he retreats.

What can I say to you? It's hard to be objective when I love you both so very much, but I shall try.

W. was wrong when he thought you would make him a nest. So many young men are like that. We must first give what we would like to receive. No one has an automatic right to be loved.

Many see certain shortcomings in the girls they court, but they are firmly convinced that when they get married, a metamorphosis will take place, and this girl to whom they are attracted will automatically become the warm, caring wife they had always dreamed about.

Only if there is a spiritual dimension in your marriage can this inner strength be set free. "If you do not know how to talk to God together, you will not be able to talk to each other," Klaus Hess, our spiritual father, told us. I know that you began your marriage with this dimension. You visited different churches looking for a church home, but then when you got home, you tore them apart. Again I remember what Klaus Hess told us: "There is no perfect church, and even if there were, it would cease to be perfect as soon as I became a member of it."

Do you remember, Ann, when we worked together on an article entitled "How to Really Love Your Husband"? We cited Walter's words that there are three things every man needs, "Praise, food, and rest." "I could live with that," your husband said. It takes a confident woman to be able to praise her husband honestly, but only when she is able to do that will he be able to fill up the holes in her heart.

I asked W. what hurt him the most after you left. He said it was looking at the garden you had planted—the shrubs, the trees, and thinking of all the love you had put into it. I think of all the gardening that goes into our marriages. On the wedding day a little tree is planted. Then it is given good soil, watered, fertilized. That takes times and effort, but if we neglect to do it, the tree is likely to die. How unutterably sad, on the day of divorce, to see the marriage tree cut down or pulled out by the roots.

I love you, Ann, and hold you in my heart.

Ingma

One of my nieces, who had experienced deep suffering when her husband left her, shared with me this Chinese proverb, which she said helped give her comfort and perspective: "Two tears were floating down a river together. One said mournfully to the other, 'I am the tear of the woman who lost her lover.' The second responded, 'I am the tear of the woman who found him.'"

Her husband got a divorce and soon married another woman. Though my niece knew the decision was out of her hands, and though she knew that without commitment no problem could be solved, she still could not escape those self-accusations: "If only I had. . . " "Why didn't I. . . " "I could have. . . "

She had to face the truth, that truth which would set her free from spinning her wheels and help her get on with life: Sin is a constant, problems continue, a new "lover" is not perfect. As long as we live in a fallen state, we will not escape problems by changing partners or settings or jobs. Our only hope is to experience what Paul describes in 2 Cor. 5:17: "Therefore, if anyone is in Christ, he is a new creation; the old has gone, the new has come" (NIV).

Coping with the Loss of a Love

"Grief is the price we pay for loving," a young widow wrote after losing her husband unexpectedly after only seventeen years of marriage. To grieve, which means literally, "to be burdened by sorrow," is only a part of the mourning process, but it is an essential part. Until "grief work" is done, we cannot go on.

Grief that is not dealt with can keep a person from being fully alive. I recall a conversation I had with a German pastor and his second wife during one of our marriage retreats. The pastor's first wife had died unexpectedly after a marriage of twenty-five years. Despite his despair, he had appeared unmoved, even stoical at her funeral. His children and his friends were worried because he refused to grieve. When he remarried less than a year later, they breathed a sigh of relief. Perhaps now all would be well.

But all was not well. Three years later, at our retreat, the pastor and his second wife were asked to share with each other their answers to the questions, What united us the most? What separates us the most? The wife was very frank when she told her husband that she felt a barrier of separation between them because he had never been able to share with her his grief at losing his first wife.

I talked with the two of them, and as we shared, a miracle took place. With tears in his eyes, speaking hesitantly at first, the pastor began to tell us about the deep sadness that had enveloped him like a fog when his first wife died. The pain and grief he had kept hidden deep in his heart came bubbling to the surface. His body shook as he tried to describe his feeling. This strong man, this spiritual leader, cried—and so did we. Now a time of cleansing and binding up could take place. The long-delayed healing process had begun.

It is not enough to place a Band-Aid on a grieving heart and hope that all will be well. The pain has to be expressed. My aunt, who lost her husband after fifty years of marriage, told me her secret for handling grief. She lived alone, and when the pain became too great, she simply went into her coat closet and screamed. She felt better after that and went on with living.

My heart was heavy one day because I was concerned about one of our children. I shared this sadness with my husband. As I rested my head in his lap, he stroked my hair and said, "Ingrid, just let the deep pain hurt."

Two days later, on a clear October morning, Walter died of heart failure in our little home in the foothills of the Austrian Alps. My world stopped that day. More than a dozen years have passed, and I still remember Walter's quiet wisdom: "Just let the deep pain hurt."

"Blessed are those who mourn, for they shall be comforted," the Bible says. In order to be comforted, we must let ourselves mourn.

I now recognize the stages of grief as similar to what John Steinbeck described when he wrote to the widow of his publisher, "After seeming cut off and alone, you will be able to pick up a thread and draw in a string and then a rope leading back to life again." I found in my early grief that it was important simply to pick up that thread, to put one foot in front of the other and keep walking, even though the way seemed dark and frightening. The Scandinavians put it this way: "When you're in a storm, pray, but don't forget to keep rowing."

Learning to walk alone, especially after a close partnership and marriage of many years, is no easy task. It seems simpler just to give up—even to run away—than to face the pain. As one couple who had been married fifty-eight years wrote to me, "It is not death that we are afraid of, but the grief that one of us must face alone."

In January 1986 the publisher Harold Shaw died after a long battle with lung cancer. His wife, Luci, grieved deeply. Losing her partner was like "radical surgery, like being cut in half," she said. "But I'm learning to welcome the pain and not dodge it. Pain teaches us what is real and what is temporal, what is superficial and what is deep. I'm trying to let pain do its work in me."[6]

I have tried to accept the refining work of pain without wallowing in self-pity. In my grief it has helped to think of others—like my mother and grandmother—who faced even greater burdens than I did after the death of their husbands.

Remorse is just as much of a dead end as self-pity. A nagging inner voice may repeat, "Why didn't I insist that he go to the doctor? Why didn't I give him that word of praise or encouragement? Now it's too late." But that's just like beating ourselves to make what has happened "unhappen." It is futile and destructive. Anne Lindbergh calls it "fooling yourself, feeding on an illusion; just as living on memories, clinging to relics and photographs, is an illusion."[7]

Guilt will also block the grief work that must be done. It is not unusual to feel guilt after a spouse dies. But we must deal with it, then move on. I found it helpful to write down and confess to my pastor all that troubled my conscience around the time of Walter's death. Just as in our marriage Walter and I had needed those times of unburdening, of confessing that which the Holy Spirit had convicted us of, I still needed those times after his death. I knew if I was to make real progress and not just spin my wheels, I needed to place my accumulated guilt and pain at the foot of the cross and hear God's word of forgiveness.

Often in those early days of grief a painful memory would cross my mind. Unable to handle it myself, I would call a close friend, a woman of prayer. She would listen patiently to my hurt and then, with words of comfort, help me turn my eyes to Jesus, the Savior who walks through our past, our present, and our future and makes all things new. Another bleeding point was then sealed off, and I could go on.

Mourning is never easy, and it lasts longer than most people think. A poll conducted just after the Vietnam War by a journalist for a major midwestern newspaper asked this question: "How long is it normal to mourn the loss of a loved one?" The majority responded that mourning is complete within forty-eight hours to two weeks after a death. Those of us who have actually walked through that valley know that two weeks is only the beginning.

Mourning is that journey which takes us from where we were before our loss to where we'll be once we've struggled to adapt to the change in our lives. No one can quite measure when those days are over. Dietrich Bonhoeffer expressed it well: "Nothing can make up for the absence of someone whom we love. And it would be wrong to try to find a substitute. . . . It is nonsense to say that God fills the gap; he does not fill it, but on the contrary, he keeps it empty and so helps us to keep alive our former communion with each other, even at the cost of pain."

Yet only one who has learned to live alone after a great loss can move into a complete relationship with others. It is a trap for a bereaved person to think that a new partner will fulfill his or her deepest needs. Don't make a major decision for at least twelve months after the death of your spouse, is wise advice. As Judith Fabisch has said, "If a widow can't readjust to living with herself, she certainly can't be effective in solving the problems of others. . . . On the other hand, remarriage is the highest praise one can pay to a deceased mate, for it says, in effect, marriage is good and I want to be part of that good relationship again."[8]

We never honor the dead by dying with them. Walter's work was finished, but God's work is not. I can honor Walter's memory best by being God's servant and steward, by living for him and for others. A support group—I like to call them a circle of lovers—can help people with losses learn the art of reaching out to others.

The great poet Rabbi Joshua Liebman put it this way: "The melody that the loved one played upon the piano of your life will never be played quite that way again, but we must not close the keyboard and allow the instrument to gather dust. We must seek out other artists of the spirit, new friends who gradually will help us find the road of life again, who will walk that road with us."[9]

Physical Helps in Grief Work

On a very practical level, how well we handle grief will depend, more than we may realize, on such things as maintaining an adequate, balanced diet and getting enough sleep and exercise. A significant weight gain or loss during a time of grief is likely to set off both physiological and emotional problems. Mourners need to watch calories—sometimes making sure they get enough—and eat balanced, nutritious foods. We also need to drink more fluids than we might think necessary. How grateful I was whenever a friend made me a simple cup of tea! During those first weeks after my loss, a tightness constricted my throat almost constantly. The tea helped.

Walking briskly for at least twenty minutes each day and swimming once or twice a week helped me control depression. I could walk or swim away from my troubles for a short time. When I was finished and had to face them again, I was able to do so with more happiness and alertness. Later, at night, my body was tired from the exercise and more ready for the sleep that often eluded me. I made a strong effort to maintain some pattern of rest, even though there were many restless nights.

Eventually I found that living at peace with myself involved discovering anew the joy of my five senses.

Touch. How wonderful it was to have the wind rush across my face or the rain fall on bare skin. How comforting it felt as I swam, completely surrounded by water, carried by it, even caressed by it.

Sight. God opened my eyes to see again. Instead of shades of gray, I began to see everything in technicolor. I saw the overwhelming beauty of nature, the miracle of a new baby, even the loveliness of age and wrinkles.

Taste. How delicious were the meals prepared by others and after a time by me, when I could once again use cooking to show my family and friends that I loved and appreciated them.

Hearing. I received healing as I listened to the great requiems of the masters, who reminded me that after the suffering of the Crucifixion comes the joy of the Resurrection.

Smell. Happy memories and innocent joys were released at the fragrance of peonies, baked apples, a breast-fed baby, clean linens, fresh coffee.

The Pain of Rejection and Failure

The confident woman can take rejection because she knows that there is one who will never reject her. She may need to grieve a while, for that is the appropriate action after any kind of loss, including rejection.

She will remember that there are only two kinds of people: those who love so that they will be loved, and those who love because they are loved. She can go on her way stronger, yes, even thankful that she is still free to pursue his will. "God gives only the best to those who leave the choice with Him." This could be a paraphrase of Rom. 8:28: "And we know that in all things God works for the good of those who love him, who have been called according to his purpose" (NIV).

I was impressed when I saw Margaret Thatcher being interviewed in the States after she had to step down as prime minister. When asked how she coped with the situation, she said, "You don't squeal. In other words, you don't complain—you cope." And just how would she do that? "By seeking to gather people together, both thinkers and doers, who believe as I do. And then I will get on with my life." Mrs. Thatcher is now Lady Thatcher of Kesteven and has joined the House of Lords, Britain's upper chamber. Her fellow peers cheered after the Iron Lady was sworn in.

I asked a well-known German psychotherapist if he could tell me the secret of his great wisdom. "Yes," he said, "I have learned the most from all the foolish mistakes I have made." A friend who is an engineer and building up his own company said, "You can only make good decisions by sometimes making bad decisions. True wisdom is not to be afraid of making mistakes. We call that risk taking, and without risk taking nothing new would be created. And what if there is a disaster? There will always be plenty of them in life, and the best thing is if we learn to celebrate them."

One *Peanuts* cartoon shows Sally sitting at a table with two pieces of paper—one large and one small—in front of her. As she writes diligently on the large piece, she says to Charlie Brown, "I'm making a list of all the things I've learned in life. . . . Well, actually I'm making two lists." Charlie Brown asks, "Why is one list longer than the other?" Holding up the long list, Sally says, "These are the things I've learned the hard way!"[10]

Experience often means failure. How can we acknowledge our failures without becoming trapped by them? Just think of them as part of the learning process. As the line of the old hymn reads, "Each victory will help you some other to win." We now have wisdom for our next battle, having learned from both our failures and our successes.

Making Sense Out of Suffering

My niece wrote me, "I hope you are dealing with the truth of identifying ourselves with Christ especially in suffering, because that has been the only real source of peace and healing for me. The better I know him, the less I hurt."

The apostle Paul, who certainly had more than his share of well-documented sufferings, declared, "I consider that our present sufferings are not worth comparing with the glory that will be revealed in us" (Rom 8:18, NIV).

"Faith is not merely receiving from God what we want. It sometimes involves accepting what he gives without doubting him," says John B. Pearrell in "Where Is God When I'm Hurting?"

Because of faulty theology, we have come to believe that God wants us all healthy and wealthy. The Bible never promises us that as Christians we are exempt from trials and suffering by

Christ's death. . . . Jesus said, "In this world you will have trouble" (John 16:33). And Paul wrote, "I want to know Christ and the power of his resurrection," but the rest of the verse says, "and the fellowship of sharing in his sufferings, becoming like him in his death." (Phil. 3:10, NIV).[11]

We humans will never be able to make complete sense out of the mystery of suffering. There are times when we need to shoulder the burdens of others, but if we continue to carry these burdens, we will become depressed. We need to cast them into the arms of our Father. We hold the pain only long enough to enable the one who is suffering to let go of it. Together we release it to God.

In his book on prayer Richard Foster tells of a young woman, a pastor's daughter, who came to him with a heavy heart. She was unhappy about her father's frequent absence because of the demands of his ministry, the tight budget, which meant few toys, skimpy vacations, no special things, and parishioners who were picky.

Richard tells this moving experience:

After she finished her sharing, I stood behind her, gently placing my hands on her head in a ritual form of the laying on of hands. I wanted to pray for the healing of the little girl still inside this woman, the little girl who had suffered all these losses. But I could speak only a few words, for I felt a deep sorrow welling up within me for her emotional pain. I prayed for forgiveness for the father who didn't know what he had done. But by then I could no longer speak, for a great brokenness came over me, and I quietly sobbed on her behalf. Emotion does not come to me quickly. . . . I entered into her pain, repented for her father, and sought healing for her inner child of the past. Evidently the tears did what the words could not, for she left substantially healed. This way of prayer we learn only in the school of suffering.[12]

Because women have a potential for motherhood, they also, I believe, have a deep sense of compassion. Men can achieve this compassion through their being wounded in the battle with evil. Jesus Christ is our great example here. He stands as the Lamb of God, the one who was slain in order to confront and conquer death itself. It is from his side that the church was born and from his wounds that the Holy Spirit flows forth. It is through him that our hearts are enlarged and even sensitized by suffering. We become wounded healers, as Henri Nouwen has formulated it. We have no pat answers. We simply enter into the pain of others.

We're not talking here about some kind of religious masochism. This is the kind of suffering that has purpose and meaning. We are glad to suffer for our children's sakes, depriving ourselves of things so that they will have a better chance at life. Maybe that's why teenage rebellion is so hard for us. We're afraid our sacrifices might be in vain.

One of my prize possessions made by my favorite aunt is a counted cross-stitch sampler of the Serenity Prayer: "Lord, give me the courage to change the things I can change, to accept the things I cannot change, and the wisdom to know the difference." There are things in our lives over which we have no control. All we can do is accept them. We don't need to pronounce judgment on them or try to justify them. "In acceptance lieth peace."

On the other hand there are things that we can change. We become guilty if we do not take on this responsibility. We deny our dignity as sons and daughters of God. This change begins within ourselves, and it usually begins with forgiveness.

Wisdom is the ability to make sound, practical judgments. It is the faculty to discern what is right and true. In simple language, it is common sense. Seldom is there wisdom in knowledge. Rather the one is wise who has taken knowledge and made it personal. That one who is able to give truth back to you through insight and discernment is a wise person. Real wisdom comes from life experience. It comes from contemplation, from mulling things over, and then seeing the truth behind it all.

The confident woman is not afraid of suffering. She knows that the best is yet ahead and that the sufferings of this present time will seem insignificant as she keeps her eyes on the goal.

❀ 10 ❀

Goals and Guidance

Many contemporary women are unsettled because they are unsure of their goals. Once we have a glimpse of our ultimate goal, which is to know God and enjoy him forever, according to the Westminster Catechism, then we can better handle our short-term goals. There is an overwhelming freedom in living within bounds.

For a Christian every goal is related to God's will. When someone asks Mother Teresa for advice, she says simply, "Do what Jesus would do." Often when a person asks me for counsel, I turn the question around, "What do you think the gentle Shepherd is telling you?"

Can We Know God's Will?

"But how can we hear the voice of the gentle Shepherd?" you ask. The psalmist says, "He guides me in paths of righteousness for his name's sake," (Ps. 23:3), and again, "Teach me to do your will, for you are my God; may your good Spirit lead me on level ground" (Ps. 143:10).

Let me share a personal experience whose implications are just now becoming clear.

In 1977 Walter was invited to speak to an All-African Conference of Pastors at Bouaké, Ivory Coast. He declined because of a full schedule. The theme was "The Christian Family," and he preferred that our African co-workers, Jean and Ernestine Banyolak, take his place.

But on his way to Austria, he recalled,

> I suddenly had the feeling this step was wrong. When I landed in Salzburg ten hours later, I still had this feeling: "I shouldn't be here. I'm in the wrong place." When I got home, I found a letter from Bouaké which undergirded this feeling. It contained an urgent and repeated invitation, together with a check for my travel expenses and the program of the conference. I discovered that it was not a question of only one lecture as I had anticipated, but they had given me four of the morning sessions of a six-day conference.
>
> I knew at once that this would be too much of a burden for Jean and Ernestine. On the spot, I decided to fly back to Africa. I arrived at the conference grounds exactly half an hour before my first lecture was to begin, just enough time to have prayer with Jean and Ernestine and plan our teamwork. Right on time, all three of us stood on the platform.[1]

Now I see the implication of Walter's obedience to God's guidance at that time. Key leaders from all over Africa attended this conference as Walter shared his vision that a message for families is the best landing strip for the gospel today. Many theological students were also in attendance.

Recently I spent three weeks in Abidjan, on the west coast of Africa. Night after night I spoke to hundreds of eager couples and singles who wanted to hear about the secrets of Christian family life. When I talked to their pastors, they told me, "We heard your husband in 1977 and have read all your books. Now we want you to share this great message with our people." If Walter had not been obedient to God's call, then perhaps the doors would not have been open for me to share in this way.

Walter once wrote a letter to his friends about how we can know God's will. Here is the gist of what he said.

1. Often guidance will become clear when we take a concrete step in a certain direction. All at once a still, small voice speaks to us gently in our hearts and we know, "I am going in the right direction," or "This step is wrong." According to 1 Kings 19:12, the Lord was not in the strong wind or the earthquake or the fire—all very dramatic occurrences. He spoke in a sound of gentle stillness. This sound cannot be heard from the outside. Only those who have inner antennae and who stop and listen in their quiet time will be able to know God's guidance.

2. If the inner antennae have received the message, then you must follow it through without looking to the left or right, without paying attention to the way the wind blows. "He who observes the wind [and waits for all conditions to be favorable] will not sow; and he who regards the clouds will not reap" (Eccles. 11:4). The outward circumstances are always ambiguous and can only be interpreted correctly in the light of the still, small voice. This sign, which is outside our control, is infallible.

It is like the needle of a compass that shows us the direction we should take, or like the directions given from the control tower when a plane is landing. We can hear a small voice telling us, "This is not right for you. Hands off." Or we hear, "This is a good opportunity for you. Try it."

3. The art of letting oneself be guided also includes the readiness to be corrected. It is humiliating to admit before God, before oneself, and before others, "I made a mistake," "I was wrong." Significantly enough, in Ps. 119:67 and 71, we read twice about humiliation. This is Martin Luther's translation, "Before I was afflicted [humiliated], I went astray" (v. 67). "It was good for me that I was afflicted [humiliated] that I might learn thy statutes" (v. 71). To accept humiliation is part of the learning process in the art of finding God's guidance.

To perceive and then to decide—God does not show us the whole way but only the next step. His promise is "I will counsel you with my eye upon you" (Ps. 32:8).

Doing God's Will

"But isn't that terribly difficult? Even if you do know God's will for your life, where do you get the strength to do it, to be obedient?" I can hear you asking.

The answer is simple. It depends on whether you will try to do it in your own strength or in God's strength. I like an analogy made by Madame Guyon, a French Christian who lived at the end of the seventeenth century, the author of a spiritual classic entitled *Experiencing the Depths of Jesus Christ*. When sailors first take a ship out of port, she wrote, it is very difficult to head it out to sea. They must use all their strength to get the ship clear of the harbor. But once the ship is at sea, it moves easily in whatever direction the seamen choose.

Christians are like that ship, she said. At first we are strongly bound by sin and by self. Only by a great deal of repeated effort are the ropes that bind us set loose.

As we are obedient, gradually we push off from the port of self. Leaving it far behind, we head for the deep sea. The farther we go from port, the easier it is to move the ship. Then comes the moment when it can use the sails, and all the pilot has to do is spread the sails and hold the rudder, thereby keeping the swiftly moving vessel gently on its course.

"*To spread the sails* is to lay yourself before God in simple prayer. 'To spread the sails' is to be moved by his Spirit.

'*To hold the rudder*' is to keep your heart from wandering away from its true course. "To hold the rudder" is to recall the heart, gently. You guide it firmly by the moving of the Spirit of God."[2]

Madame Guyon says that as our Lord gains possession of our hearts and we move into him, it is like the gentle breeze filling the sails and moving the ship forward.

"When the winds are favorable, the pilot rests from his work. The pilot rests and leaves the ship to be moved by the wind. . . . They are making more progress in one hour without any effort than they ever did before, even when exerting all their strength. . . . If God is your mover, you will go much farther in a short time than all your repeated self-effort could ever do."[3]

At the end of her little book, Madame Guyon says: "Follow the counsel of Paul: Allow yourself to be led by the Spirit of God. That Spirit will unerringly conduct you to the end purpose for which your soul was created. That end purpose is the enjoyment of God."[4]

Setting Goals

In order to carry out God's will as we understand it, we can set goals in three areas: spiritual, personal, and vocational.

Spiritual Goals

If we are to have our spiritual goals clear, we must work on inner order. To do that we look into God's mirror, the Ten Commandments. Pastor Herbert Fuchs who married us, wrote them down in this modern form and called them The Questionnaire of God. Here they are.

1. Which person or what thing is more important to you than God? What do you think about the first thing in the morning and the last thing at night?
2. Are you guided in your thinking and actions by superstitious ideas? Do fortune-tellers, horoscopes, spiritism, and magic arts influence your life or those who live with you?
3. When you make plans and decisions, do you seek God's will? Do you take enough time to listen to God's word, or do you try to escape it through work and pleasure?
4. With whom do you have strained relationships? Within or outside your family are there those to whom you are indifferent or toward whom you feel reproach and scorn? Are you ready to take responsibility over and above your personal field of activity?

5. Is there someone who may have wronged you and whom you cannot forgive and then forget (the problem)? Do you try to help others outwardly or inwardly, or do you look for help only for yourself?

6. Is God's commandment the standard for you in sexual questions, not only in relationship with others but also in regard to yourself? Where do you see the root of your failure in this field?

7. Have you illegally taken something for your own or not returned something you borrowed? What do you possess that you don't really need but that someone else needs badly? Does God receive his share of your earnings?

8. To whom have you lied? Whom have you judged deliberately, falsely, or unkindly, either by written or spoken word?

9. Whom do you secretly envy because of his or her personal appearance, reputation, position, abilities, or possessions? Can you rejoice with someone who has more than you, or do you become bitter when you compare yourself with such a person?

10. Are you ready to receive everything as entrusted to you from God, even that which you do not understand and which is not according to your personal desires? Do the words *good luck* and *bad luck* occur in your vocabulary?

When I first considered these questions, I wrote down my answers to each one and then went to an older woman, my prayer partner, who could counsel me spiritually. She assured me of Christ's words, "Whoever comes to me, I will never drive away" (John 6:37b, NIV). She reminded me of the promise in 1 John 1:9: "If we confess our sins, he is faithful and just and will forgive us our sins."

Personal and Vocational Goals

There is no conflict between faith and goal setting. I believe that God has goals for all of us. The apostle Paul certainly believed in goal setting when he said, "Forgetting what is behind and straining toward what is ahead, I press on toward the goal" (Phil. 3:13b, 14, NIV).

One way that we can discern our goals is to sit down and answer the following questions suggested by Father Basil Pennington at a spiritual retreat I attended:

1. What do I want?
2. What do I need to do to get what I want and to know I have it or am on the way to getting it?
3. What are the obstacles? What prevents me from getting it done?
4. Am I charting my progress—daily, weekly, monthly? Have I had a personal retreat (half a day) once a month and check up on myself?

When I asked my pastor how he defined a confident woman, he said, "She knows where she's going. She's got her orders straight." Then he gave me this wonderful definition of *submission:* in Latin it means "one who is sent under orders." I believe that when we listen to the gentle Shepherd, he also guides us in our personal goals. God wants only the best for us. He likes to treat each one of us as if we were an only child. We can put our "hope in God, who richly provides us with everything for our enjoyment" (1 Tim. 6:17, NIV).

Eve, the mother of all the living, thought she was missing something. If she ate of the tree of the knowledge of good and evil, then she would be wise and confident. She deliberately disobeyed and said no to God's plan. The result was sin, disorder, and confusion.

Mary, on the other hand, said yes to God's plan. When confronted with the message of the angel that she was to be the mother of Jesus, she said simply, "I am the Lord's servant. May it be to me as you have said." She placed her body, mind, and spirit at the disposal of the Lord, thereby making her the great "Yes-sayer" to his plan. Her trust in God was so great that she was not afraid of what man would say, including her betrothed. She truly is our model of "one who is sent under orders."

Our pastor warned us about the off-balance teachings about submission that can be an excuse for women to remain passive and to cop out from becoming whole persons. Indecision and inaction on our part can actually be a subtle way of controlling those who live with us.

Margaret, who shares my home, is a divorcée in her early fifties. She has four adult children. When I asked her about her personal goals, she answered without hesitation: get out of debt and establish a financial plan; do some kind of "hands-on" missionary work; learn to play a musical instrument.

When asked what she would like to do, a retired nurse replied, "Volunteer work with children. Most day-care centers are understaffed. I would like to be a backup in a child-care unit. Not only would I find that very satisfying, but it would also give me a reason for getting up in the morning."

In our congregation there is a woman in her mid-eighties who loves children. Every Sunday she sits at the entrance of the Sunday school rooms. There she greets every child who enters and tells them how happy she is to see them. She also notices when children are absent, and they are doubly welcome when they return. Being able to do this is a fulfillment of her goal to be useful in God's Kingdom.

Each one of us has gifts. It often takes a lifetime to discover all our gifts and put them to use. We need to ask God to show us where our gifts are needed, because that is where we can best serve him.

Søren Kierkegaard once said, "Each one of us needs a purpose for which he is ready to live and to die." When I heard this, I asked myself, What am I ready to live and die for? Without hesitation I knew my goal: to be an instrument in helping release couple power. What is couple power? It's the multiplied power of two whole people joined as man and wife. Two people together can do more than two separately, especially when they know that as man and woman they have been created in the image of God. Together they mirror his image to the world.

But first of all we need single power. This means for me that both our masculine and feminine sides need to be developed if we are to reflect God's image to a broken world.

I also knew that to be effective in this work, I would need more vocational training. My first goal was to take the same course that my husband had taken in marriage and family counseling in Los Angeles. But how could I do this when I had five children between the ages of eight and sixteen and we lived in Austria? I talked it over with Walter. Instead of telling me that my dream was impossible, he set about making a plan. I would take the two youngest children with me to the States, where they could stay with relatives when I was in classes. Walter meanwhile would take our three teenagers on a six-week camping trip through France, Italy, and Yugoslavia.

Taking this course was the foundation for lifelong learning in this field. Every year I have been able to supplement what I learned there with training workshops as well as with new books in the field. This together with in-depth experience in working with couples throughout the world has helped me realize both my personal and vocational goals.

One of my sisters enrolled in nurses' training when she was forty years old and her youngest child was in middle school. It took a lot of stretching, both on her part and on the part of her family, but she reached her goal. As a result she has had a useful and fulfilling career as a nurse, and this in turn has enhanced her ministry as a pastor's wife.

Other women I know have gone back to college to finish a degree or to get an advanced degree in theology, medicine, education.

One of my cousins, who lost her husband through a tragic accident, began her teaching career when her own children started school. Each year she writes to me at Christmas telling of her life as a single mother and her satisfaction in her work. This last Christmas she wrote to me:

> My own teaching becomes less academic and more "grand-mothering" each year as the little ones come to school with such enormous emotional needs. They don't know how to talk to each other or share. In a room full of potential friends, many choose to work and play alone. I suppose it seems "safest" to them. In your work you see couples who find it hard to love each other, and I see the results—children who can't love themselves and are afraid to risk communicating with others. If someone invades their space, they hit or pick or scream. These children are not coming to school ready to learn.
>
> There are, of course, some who shine like beacons through all this gloom. There is always hope!

It's always been an encouragement to me to know that God does the calling. Jesus said to his disciples, "You did not choose me, but I chose you and appointed you to go and bear fruit—fruit that will last" (John 15:16, NIV).

Fruit bearing is not something that we can do on our own. As Anne Ortlund, author and speaker, has written: "The quality of your life will be determined by the amount of time you spend alone with God—reading, praying and planning."

❀ 11 ❀

Use of Time

Time is a finite wealth that each of us has received at birth, and it is there for us to spend and invest. If we are realistic, we see that there are no deposits involved in time, only withdrawals.

Having goals is like having a road map. The next step is to use the time allotted to us to reach these goals. In her current circumstances my youngest daughter, Ruth, a physician, illustrates this. She recently wrote to me, "Because I now know what my goal is, I can enjoy my children so much more." She is using this time when her sons are small to prepare for her future specialty in medicine, one step at a time.

Losing No Shred of Time

John Wesley, the great Christian leader in England (1703–1791), warned his people about the danger of sins of omission: "Sins of omission are avoiding to do good of any kind when we have the opportunity. . . . Do all the good you possibly can to the bodies and souls of your neighbors. Be active. Give no place to laziness. Be always busy, *losing no shred of time.*"

What does "losing no shred of time" mean for the confident woman? Keeping an easy rhythm between work and play. Changing pace—going from intellectual work to gardening, cleaning, cooking. My mother-in-law, Gertrud, was a teacher for ten years before she married and had three children. She told me that it was a difficult adjustment for her, that first year out of the classroom. She learned that she could have a book of poems above her sink and be memorizing poetry while she peeled potatoes. Anne Lindbergh, in her wonderful book *Gift from the Sea*, said, "And when I cannot write a poem, I bake biscuits and feel just as pleased."[1] Physical tasks can balance life in a refreshing way.

Sometimes by changing our place of activity we can also make better use of time. It gives me a lift to leave my desk and go sit on the front porch with a cup of tea when I read the daily mail. Even Winston Churchill used to entice his tired secretaries as they followed him from London to Malta to Potsdam and back to London, with this statement, "A change is as good as a rest."

We need to be in touch with time, not only in terms of what time of day it is but also for the constructive use of time. "Quit spending your time. Invest it." A built-in alarm system within us causes feelings of remorse when we waste time. Now that I am in my midsixties I am very conscious that I no longer have unlimited time. I want to use this warning system within not so much to feel ashamed when I waste time as to say yes to that healthy anxiety that will better help me to use my "nows" and "future nows."

George MacDonald gives us this good advice: "In my labor I am content to do the thing that lies next to me. In all of life, there is nothing so significant as the next five minutes and whether we use it to do what God lays before us." May we all learn to do this without losing our peace, for as Amy Carmichael has said, "To lose our peace is to lose our power to help. The energies which might have been turned to power are wasted in effectless grieving."

The great secret is learning to do the right thing at the right time. The prophet says, "He will teach us what he wants us to do. We will walk in the paths he has chosen" (Mic. 4:2, TEV). "See that you do all the work you were given to do as the Lord's servant" (Col. 4:17, NRSV). Another translation of Paul's words is, "Fulfill your ministry" (RSV).

Julia von Bodelschwingh, whose husband was director of Bethel, the largest Christian institution in the world for mentally and physically disabled people, wrote these words about her daily life after the death of her husband, "I don't know which way to go and it's the same story every morning. But one thing I do know and that is to take little steps. Steps which are short enough and yet long enough so that God is visible to my eyes and so that He can light up my path."[2]

An efficiency expert tells plant supervisors, "Finish one big job and one little job every day." Instead of having your desk cluttered with unfinished projects, choose the one that can be finished and do it. Eleanor Roosevelt said in her biography, "If I have something to do, I just do it." When asked how she managed to get so much done, she said, "I don't waste time on regrets." A German friend gave me this advice, "Don't meditate reproaches."

Restfully Busy

I asked my eleven-year-old friend Simeon if he didn't need a watch. Wouldn't that help him get to school on time? "No," he said, "I don't want a watch, because if I looked at it, I'd have to hurry." "A lady never hurries," I was told in Africa.

I like the term *restfully busy,* which Paul White in Australia, author of the *Jungle Doctor* book series, uses to end his Christmas letters. Although he is in his eighties, he continues to be involved in many new projects each year. Restfully busy gives me a different feeling of living with time than "hurry-hurry" does.

Are we able to live without hurrying? It's certainly hard to be sensitive, to be able to listen, in a hurry-hurry situation. Hurry is one of the deadliest enemies of the spirit. It is crowded anxiety, a lack of assurance that God is in control. This is just the opposite of what the psalmist says: "Commit your way to the Lord; trust in him and he will act. . . . Be still before the Lord, and wait patiently for him" (Ps. 37:4, 7, RSV). "I will lie down and sleep in peace, for you alone, O Lord, make me dwell in safety." (Ps. 4:8 NIV).

Jesus was not in a hurry. He took time each day to get his instructions from his Father. We cannot hurry either in the discipline of our spiritual life. Only when we take time to listen to the voice of the gentle Shepherd will we be enabled to do the things we cannot do alone. If we try to hurry-hurry our prayer life, we can make it irrelevant. It would be like baking a cake and being too busy to put in the vanilla and the eggs. What kind of a cake would that be?

Sometimes I need to admit that I cannot finish some task. I can only do today what I can do today. Therefore I'm going to leave this job unfinished. Discipleship is learning to live my life as he would like me to. He is the only one who knows the end from the beginning. Therefore I cannot afford not to take time to listen to him and then obey what he says.

Here are some rules that work for me:

1. Take a "power nap." It does wonders and can be as short as five or ten minutes. I say to myself those words of Jesus that I believe he meant especially for women, "Come to me, all you who are weary and burdened, and I will give you rest. Take my yoke upon you and learn from me, for I am gentle and humble in heart, and you will find rest for your souls" (Matt. 11:28, 29, NIV). I add to it the promise God gave Moses in Exod. 33:14, "My presence will go with you and I will set your mind at rest." That takes care of rest for body, mind, and soul. Instead of stress, he wants to give us rest.

2. Make yourself a cup of tea and ask the Lord to show you "the next indicated step." That's a term I got from one of my brothers, who is an accountant. Sometimes that means doing the least desirable task first. But sometimes this is like getting a cork out of a bottle; the rest starts to flow and falls into place.

3. Divide and conquer. I break down the big mountain into little mountains. Another name for this is the "Swiss

cheese approach," which really means making little holes in a big project. Or, as an editor once told me, "You can only eat an elephant one bite at a time." Occasionally someone will ask me, "What can I do to help?" And then I apply the rule, "Never put off until tomorrow what you can delegate today."

4. Cut off escape routes that might make it easy to abandon your task. My son is using my car today, which leaves me here at my desk with no excuses. Besides that, my co-workers prayed that God would put a "hedge" around me until I finish this chapter.

5. Give yourself a reward for finishing a task or a part of the task. Hurrah—I made it! I'm going for a refreshing swim in my favorite Ozark lake and afterward a picnic on the dock, watching the sun go down.

Patience

I recently received a letter from my daughter Katrine, who is living one of the most intense chapters of her life as the wife of a diplomat and mother of five. She wrote down her thoughts on patience, something she's learned a lot about from her youngest daughter, Margaret, who has Down's syndrome. I've asked Katrine's permission to share her thoughts with you:

Love Is Patient *(1 Cor. 13:4)*

Patience is waiting.
Patience is waiting, is Advent.
Patience is waiting for a child to be born.
Patience is the love of God.
Patience is a slow-blooming flower, modest and
    full of promise.
Patience knows how to be still and listen.
Patience is gentle and sweet.
Patience understands the beauty of quiet inner
    growth that cannot be hurried.

Patience chases away pressure and stress.

Patience can never be overwhelmed.

Patience teaches the art of living with unfulfilled desires.

Patience is serene and tranquil.

Patience is a motherly virtue.

Patience is winter waiting for spring.

Patience is the thawing of a frozen heart.

Patience is taking one step at a time.

Patience is renouncing control.

Patience is running with perserverance the race.

Patience does not seek rest. It provides rest.

Patience is our reserve fuel when the tank runs empty.

It will carry us safely to our destination.

Patience is fasting.

Patience is starting all over again.

Patience is rejoicing on a Monday morning.

Patience is the continuous process of uncluttering what is around you and inside you.

Patience is committing yourself in faith to God's plan for you.

Patience is longing without receiving.

Patience creates room where there is no room.

Patience creates time where there is no time.

Patience keeps on striving without tangible results.

Patience is potty-training Margaret.

Patience keeps on praying.

Patience keeps on keepin' on.

Patience is living an ocean away.

Patience is looking for a lost treasure.

Patience is living with a deceitful heart.

Patience is living with unanswered questions.

The eyes of Christ are full of *patience* as He looks into our eyes.

We need this perspective that Katrine describes from her own life. The art is to look beyond the smallness of this present moment and see it in relationship to eternity. At the same time we live and enjoy to the fullest the sacrament of the present moment.

Holy Leisure

What is time for? If it is only for work, then what will be left of me when the work is gone?

A story is told about one of the Desert Fathers, Abba Anthony. One day a hunter in the desert saw Abba Anthony enjoying himself with the brethren and he was shocked. What kind of spiritual guide was this?

But the old monk said to him, "Put an arrow in your bow and shoot it." So the hunter did. Then the old man said, "Now shoot another." So the hunter did. Then the elder said, "Shoot your bow again. Keep shooting; keep shooting; keep shooting." And the hunter finally said, "But if I bend my bow so much I will break it."

Then Abba Anthony said to him, "It is just the same with the work of God. If we stretch ourselves beyond measure, we will break. Sometimes it is necessary to meet other needs." When the hunter heard these words he was struck with remorse and, greatly edified by Anthony, he went away. As for the monastics there, they went home strengthened.[3]

I have heard that the amount of leisure time in the U.S. is decreasing rather than increasing. With our computers, fax machines, and car phones, we get more done, but we're apparently not getting more time for rest and refreshment.

Scholars of the Talmud tell us that the Sabbath is emphasized in Genesis not to show that God needed rest but to show that he created rest and he demanded that we rest on the Sabbath. The Sabbath is essential to creation for three reasons, they said.

1. It equalizes the rich and the poor. For one day a week everyone is the same—they are equally free.

2. It gives us time to evaluate our work, just as God evaluated his work on that day. Is what we are doing "good"?
3. It gives us time to contemplate the meaning of life.

Sometimes I think that my life is too filled with meaning, and I can drown in it if I cannot take time to sort it out and give it a form. One of my best friends said to me, "My life is a whole blob of meaning. That's why I need lots of time with the Lord to hear his voice and do only that which he has called me to do."

Did you ever stop to think if that one-seventh of every week is rest, then one-seventh of life is rest: 52 days a year, 3,640 days in seventy years—or ten years of Sabbath rest and reflection in a lifetime. As a college student, I learned to put this in practice by not studying or writing papers on Sunday but using that day for the Lord and for rest, recreation, and reflection. That rule probably saved me from a breakdown, for I was working more than twenty hours a week at a job and carrying sixteen and more hours of college credits. I'd like to challenge students to celebrate the Sabbath.

I learned from my busy mother that her secret of carrying on at an even tempo year after year in raising her large family was her Sunday afternoon nap. "That helps me to catch up so that I have new strength and joy for the next week," she said.

In reading the Rule of Saint Benedict, I was surprised to know that every member of the community was to spend three hours a day in reading and reflection time. Saint Benedict did not order one of the monks to be sent around the monastery to see if everyone was doing their assigned work. He did, however, make the rule that a monk should be sent around during the hours of leisure to see if the monastics were doing their reading and reflecting, which included taking walks.

Leisure has two dimensions: play and rest. We are in danger of making our play into work. We need to learn to play again if our spiritual lives are going to be healthy. As Sister Joan Chittister says: "The leisure that Benedictine spirituality deals with is holy

leisure, leisure that is for holy things, leisure that makes the human more human by engaging the heart and broadening the vision and deepening the insight and stretching the soul. Benedictine spirituality is more intent on developing thinking people than it is on developing pious people. It is one thing to pray prayer; it is another thing to be prayerful."[4]

Each morning as I begin my day, I sing an old hymn that is in the New Year section of my hymnbook. One of the verses has these words: "Our times are in Thy hand, O God, we wish them there. Our life, our friends, our souls, we leave entirely to Thy care" (E. R. Gieren).

❀ 12 ❀

Friendship with God

Many people think that if they just find the right partner, then that will solve all their problems. Over and over again I share my deep conviction with women: No man is able to satisfy the deepest longings of his wife's heart. Only one can do that—Jesus Christ. Neither can any woman satisfy the deepest longings of her husband's heart.

For me personally it has been a great help to meet with a small Renovaré group of seven whose goal is to help one another become better disciples of Jesus. *Renovaré* comes from the Latin word that means "to be made new." It is the name of the movement that Richard Foster, author and church leader, has begun in order to bring a spirit of renewal to Christians everywhere.[1] Those who are members of this movement make a covenant agreement to be obedient to these five disciplines:

1. The Prayer-filled Life
2. The Virtuous Life
3. The Spirit-filled Life
4. The Compassionate Life
5. The Word-centered Life

We do this by means of five questions that we respond to each week. The questions are simple, but they search us to the depths and call for accountability. Here are the five questions:

1. What experiences of prayer and meditation have you had this week?
2. What temptations did you face this week?
3. What movements of the Holy Spirit did you experience this week?
4. What opportunities to serve others have you had this week?
5. In what ways have you encountered Christ in your study of the Bible?

Let us look at each one of these in more detail.

1. The Prayer-filled Life

I met my neighbor on her morning walk and told her I was working on the theme "The Confident Woman."

"How does a woman become confident?" I asked her.

Without hesitation and with shining eyes she replied, "Through prayer!"

Before we can pray effectively, we need to be reminded of the promises that are given to us. Here are some of the strong passages in the Scriptures where I found the word *confidence*. The first one was from Jer. 17:7, 8 and is very much like Psalm 1. Don't mind that I have changed the gender to feminine—I learned early on from my father that when God speaks to his children in his Word, God addresses both sons and daughters.

Blessed is the woman who trusts in the Lord,
  whose *confidence* is in him.
She will be like a tree planted by the water, that sends out her
  roots by the stream.
She does not fear when heat comes;
  her leaves are always green.
She has no worries in a year of drought
  and never fails to bear fruit.

Isaiah wrote, "In quietness and confidence shall be your strength" (30:15). This promise underlines the secret of getting to know the one who can satisfy our longings, the one who says, "I have come that they may have life, and have it to the full" (John 10:10, NIV).

In the Book of Hebrews I found the word *confidence* several times:

- "We have come to share in Christ if we hold firmly till the end the *confidence* we had at first" (3:14).
- "Let us approach the throne of grace with *confidence* so that we may receive mercy and find grace to help us in time of need" (4:16).
- "Therefore, sisters, since we have *confidence* to enter the most holy place by the blood of Jesus . . . let us draw near to God with a sincere heart in full assurance of faith. . . . Let us hold unswervingly to the hope we profess, for he who promised is faithful" (10:19).
- "So do not throw away your *confidence;* it will be richly rewarded" (10:35).

In 1 John 5:13–15, we are given another sure promise: "This is the *confidence* we have in approaching God, that if we ask anything according to his will, he hears us. And if we know that he hears us—whatever we ask—we know that we have what we asked of him."

These are strong words. How do we go about claiming them? Certainly not by being puppets and expecting God to somehow manipulate the strings so that we will be magically delivered from our Sea of Despondency. Eugene Peterson in his wonderful book *Run with the Horses,* says,

God doesn't want tame pets to fondle and feed. He wants mature, free people who will respond to Him in authentic individuality. "Draw near with boldness—with confidence." He invites us.

How few of us live with quiet, inner confidence, and yet how many of us desire it. But such inward quiet is a great grace we can receive as we practice not talking. And when we have it, we may be able to help others who need it. After we know that confidence, we may, when others come fishing for reassurance and approval, send them to fish in deeper waters for their own inner quiet.[2]

Often the prayer of confidence and trust follows the cry of anguish, for in the expression of pain I consent to be honest with God, confessing the limitation of my faith, and finding, like Thomas, that the one I thought was gone now stands before me. It helps me to see how God's people in many ages and circumstances have dealt with waiting times, and remembering makes the waiting time more bearable.

The Lord has said, "I will never fail you nor forsake you." Hence we can confidently say, "The Lord is my helper, I will not be afraid" (Heb. 13:5–6).

Why are we here, wanderers on earth? When I asked my eldest son this question, his simple answer was, "To find the way back home and to help others find the way home."

2. The Virtuous Life

"You take on the image of the one you love," Bill Pearce said recently on "Nightsounds," one of the radio programs I do not like to miss. When we know his love, we will become the persons he wants us to be. He does not patch up our natural virtues but creates a new person. God made us in his image and redeemed us through Jesus Christ. God has no grandchildren; he has only children, and he treats each one of us as an only child. Only as I put my hand in his, to accept his gift of forgiveness and deep cleansing, can I walk through the day.

Just as I must plug in my hot pot when traveling if I am to have boiling water, so I plug into the power source available in Jesus Christ. I hear his word to me saying, "My power is made perfect in weakness" (2 Cor. 12:9). He enables me to reply to each temptation with silence and prayer.

There's only one condition to receiving this power. The conduit has to be clear. If the line to the power source is cut or broken, it needs to be repaired. The only way to do this is to look in God's mirror, his Word. Then let the searchlight of his Holy Spirit focus on that which needs to be cleaned up. The Ten Commandments are not the Ten Suggestions. His Word is very clear: 1 John 1:7, "If we confess our sins, he is faithful and just and will forgive us our sins." As one youth leader said, "A clean heart for a fresh start."

Once we have a fresh start through forgiveness, we can experience the "walking in the light and having fellowship with one another." The only thing that will hinder this joy is if we refuse to forgive those who may have wronged us. Then we dare not pray the Lord's Prayer, "Forgive us our trespasses as we forgive those who trespass against us."

God and you are a majority. He said to his followers, "All authority in heaven and on earth has been given me. Therefore go. . . . And surely I am with you always, to the very end of the age." Should we not then be confident?

I studied for two years in Paris in order to get my French teaching certificate before going to French Cameroon. Besides learning French, I also learned truths about my walk with the Lord. One of those truths came from Walter Trobisch, a German exchange student at Augustana Seminary, Rock Island, Illinois. We had met only briefly before I left the States. He had asked if he could correspond with me, and I was in agreement.

I had been in Paris only a few days when I received Walter's first letter. He wrote, "Ingrid, I have a message for you. I prayed for you in my Quiet Time today. Then I listened and wrote down this message: 'Tell Ingrid not to be an angel walking somewhere in the clouds, but to walk on the earth as Jesus walked and meet people where they are. Only then will she be a real missionary.'" Then he went on to explain what he meant.

"It's true, after we have been born on this earth, we have to be born again—from the natural man to the spiritual man. But God isn't finished with us. He wants us to be born a third time, back from the spiritual to just being human again."

3. The Spirit-filled Life

Have you searched the Scriptures to discover your spirit-filled life? Have you ever considered spending an hour a week nurturing those gifts? In Gal. 5:22 we read about the fruits of the Spirit: love, joy, peace, patience, gentleness, goodness, faithfulness, and self-control. Choose one of these fruits and pray for its increase in your life.

My niece told me that the hardest hour of the day for her as a divorcée whose wounds are still fresh is when she wakes up in the morning. She can face the day only when she spiritually puts on the whole armor of God, as Paul describes it in Eph. 6:14–17 as she dresses for the day. As Paul says, "Girding our loins with truth, putting on the breastplate of righteousness, having the sandals of the gospel of peace, taking the shield of faith, putting on the helmet of salvation, and taking in hand the sword of the Spirit, which is the word of God."

4. The Compassionate Life

As I pondered the question, What opportunities to serve others have I had this week? I opened my mail. There was a letter from Austria, from Beth and Arthur Domig. Theirs was the last wedding at which Walter officiated. A few short months later, they helped me with the sad task of organizing his funeral. Now they have three children and are directing the work of Family Life Mission in Austria. Here is what they wrote:

> It was a Saturday morning. The children were together in our room, lying or sitting on our bed as Arthur and I shared the news of the telephone call the night before. A Yugoslavian mother and child who had escaped from war-torn Bosnia with

only the clothes on their back were here in our village, desperate for a place to stay. A friend had asked if we might possibly have room for them. We wanted to talk it over with the children before we made any decision.

"Let's just bow our heads quietly and ask God what he would want us to do." After a few minutes of silent prayer, we asked the children what they felt God was telling them. Each child shared his ideas about how we could help. This was the plan: Daniel, twelve, would give up his new room and move again into Becky's room. That room would be more comfortable for our guests and give them easy access to the downstairs bathroom. This was a great sacrifice on Daniel's part, because he had only had his own room a few short months and was very proud of it and happy to have his own place. However, as I helped him gather together his clothes and toys, I was humbled and thankful for his positive attitude: "Actually, Mommy, I'm happy that I can do something to help these people. I hope they feel comfortable in my room."

Daniel listened to how God was directing him to be compassionate, and he acted on it. Can we do the same? Write a kind and encouraging letter to a friend, get up early and clean house, donate blood, recycle our trash, offer to help a friend who broke her wrist, prepare a meal for a new mother. These are times when actions speak louder than words.

In her article "Living Beyond the Babble," Maxine Glaz challenges women to do just this: "As women we are faithful when we protest the abuse of other women and the consequences of abuse for children. We are faithful when we offer concern and help to our neighbors, husbands or children. . . . Most of all we keep human life human by living out what we have learned about love with steadfastness and grace."[3]

5. The Word-centered Life

God is present in his Word. In southern Missouri the older Ozarkians have what they call a bed Bible. They place it on the pillow, where they read it before they go to bed. Then they place it on their shoes, where they read it when they get up.

Father Basil Pennington says that our spiritual life is like a friendship. The reading of the Word is like getting acquainted. Meditating on the Word is like going out to dinner together. Praying is like getting engaged, and contemplation is like marriage.

A word I hold on to in times of great stress and the resulting weakness that causes fear is 2 Tim. 1:9: "God did not give us a spirit of fear, but of power [confidence] and of love and of a sound mind."

I believe that the opposite of fear is confidence and joy. I do not learn this confidence and joy from fearful people who are constantly talking about all the dangers and temptations of the world. Rather I learn it from being connected to the source of power in the Word of God and from other people who rely on this source. Then I am ready to face the world.

How to Live One Day with Jesus

If we can live one day with Jesus, we can live every day with Him, each one as it comes. Immanuel, a name for Christ, means "God with us." Human life was meant to be dramatic. We are meant to be God-inhabited. Our religion is not organized around keeping God at a distance. It allows us to go see him when we want. If I really want God to be with me, then my life will be extremely different from ordinary human life. The outcome will be far greater than the efforts.

Remember how the Israelites received manna for just one day at a time? We need to remember that one day's supply is enough. This is built upon faith—that I really believe that he is in charge now, that he is with me. I also need to desire it. (We can sometimes regard Jesus as necessary but not desirable.) This experience of living close to Jesus is built on a decision, which is an inward resolve that I will do whatever is necessary to bring it to pass. This means arrangements, making plans for reaching this goal.

My husband often said, "The next day begins the night before." That meant for him going to bed early enough so that he would not have to wake up tired. And it meant laying out his clothes for the next day so there would be no time wasted searching for the right shirt or tie or his jogging suit and shoes.

Here are some suggestions Dallas Willard gave us in a workshop entitled "How to Live One Day with Jesus":

> The biblical day, God's day, begins at sundown, the early evening we might call it. God appoints an end to man's labors with darkness. . . . "Man goeth forth unto his work and to his labor until the evening" (Ps. 104:23).
>
> In darkness we gather, we recollect, we praise, we dream in the security God has given to us. Above all, we rest. Rest is an act of faith, especially today. Few people today get the rest God has appointed for their nature. If you're not rested, you are under conditions that lead to defeat. Sleep is an expression of faith.[4]

It is good to settle all household disputes before retiring. "Let not the sun go down on your wrath." There should be "nothing between" you and your spouse, your child, your roommate.

Decide as you retire to meet with God the first thing when you awake, and go over in your mind how that will be. Fall asleep in prayer. Think of the simple prayers of childhood:

> Now I lay me down to sleep,
> I pray the Lord, my soul to keep.
> If I should die before I wake,
> I pray thee, Lord, my soul to take.

or

> Jesus, tender Shepherd hear me;
> Bless Thy little lamb tonight;
> Through the darkness be Thou near me;
> Keep me safe till morning light.

Think of the Lord's Prayer, which is really a child's prayer, or the Twenty-third Psalm. I'm going to arise and greet God and enjoy his company.

If you go to bed in faith, then it will be natural (supernatural) for you to arise with praise to God. It's very important how we awaken. This is certainly true for children. They should be awakened gently. Let them revel for a few minutes in the warmth of their blankets. One wise mother had a hard time waking up her eight-year-old boy. Then she learned to give him his special blanket and tuck it in firmly so that he had a few comforting minutes to "come to" before he had to get up.

In my bedroom I have a photograph of a fourth-century painting of Christ from the walls of the Mount Sinai monastery in Israel. The eyes of Jesus are looking at me. Sometimes they even seem to be filled with tears when I find my heart is heavy or I am grieved over a situation of one I love. At other times the eyes are twinkling with joy. The moment I wake I welcome the presence of Jesus and ask him to be with me throughout the new day. When troubles and concerns start rising from within me, I have a little pitching game. I cast them at the feet of the one who welcomes them. "Cast all your cares upon him" (1 Pet. 5:7). "If I don't cast them there, then I will be downcast," Martin Luther said.

I had a husband who was an early riser, and it was his great compassion and joy to bring me a cup of tea each morning. What wonderful memories I have of that time, of his opening the door, almost as if Jesus entered the room with the tea tray. It was our time to begin the day together by reading the Word and praying together. Then we were ready to face what might come.

Now in my widowhood, I have to do it alone—plug in the electric tea kettle and prepare tea. That first sip of tea and piece of Ry-Krisp is a symbol for me of his body and blood. I am nourished both physically and spiritually. I have confidence to begin the day.

Then it is time to hear what he has to say. After reading the Word—I like to follow the Bible reading plan of the Daily Texts of the Moravian Church[5]—I write down in my journal the answers to four questions:

1. What am I thankful for in this Word of God?
2. For what am I sorry?
3. What shall I pray for today?
4. What is my plan for this day?

A good way to remember these four steps is to use the acronym TRIP, which stands for Thanks, Repentance, Intercession, and Plan.

After a time of just sitting on my heavenly Father's lap, listening to his voice, and letting myself be loved, I am ready to face the day. I want to invite Jesus into each new situation or relationship as I move through the day. I think of John 7:37: "Whoever believes in me, as the Scripture has said, streams of living waters will flow from within him." I pray that the peace and joy that I am experiencing will pass from me like living waters to those with whom I talk. I pray a blessing for all those whom I will meet, "The Lord be gracious to you." My body is the receptacle of the Holy Spirit. That's why I want to love my body, take care of it, bless it.

Dallas Willard suggests that every two or three hours we take ten minutes to lift a fully concentrated heart and mind to God in thanksgiving and petition. Sometimes I can do this by looking at the beauty of a flower or the sky or listening to beautiful music. God has created all things to praise him.

What if I get off course? What if I fail? I just thank Jesus for being a good friend and resume my course. Don't fuss over failures. Christ doesn't, and I have better things to do than concentrate on my failures. When you learn to ski, the first thing you have to do is learn how to fall. Then you get up and try all over again. I remembered watching my children do this as their father taught them to ski.

At the end of the day, take fifteen minutes to review it. Give thanks for the successes and try to understand why any failure that occurred did occur. It's okay for us to succeed. We don't follow these disciplines in order to attain righteousness, but because they are good for us. Jean-Pierre de Caussade, who wrote the classic, *The Sacrament of the Present Moment,* said, "I feel such confidence in God that I rise above all these troubles and remain at peace when I should have expected to have been completely overwhelmed by the multitude of complicated affairs."[5]

I Have a Friend

After my oldest daughter, Katrine, visited me, I found this hand-written devotional on the desk in her room. She gave me permission to share it here. It is a message for those who love because they are loved.

"I Have a Friend"

I have a special personal friend. Some of you know this friend a little already and I'd like to share with you a few things about him. I love to call him up on the telephone. Not once have I been put on hold. Not once have I been asked to leave a message. Miraculously, he always picks up on the other end. You can't imagine how much this repeated experience has reassured me. Then I can talk to him and tell him whatever I called about. But the best part of the phone call comes when I can be completely quiet and just listen. Somehow during those moments he makes me feel extremely special. He lets me know that he delights in the times when I sit back and listen to him . . .

There are a few odd things about our friendship. For one thing, he chose me as his friend. In the beginning I did not particularly seek him out. And then he seems to see and appreciate things in me that simply aren't there. At least not yet. It is as if he loves in me what I am becoming. This kind of love is deeply troubling and convicting. I am simply not there yet, and still he loves me with a forgiving and compassionate heart every inch of the way. My friend is gracious and righteous. He takes great joy in me. He does not change like a shifting shadow. He heals my broken heart and binds up my wounds. His love and his faithfulness reach to the skies.

Even King David said hundreds of years before the telephone was invented: I love this friend of yours, Katrine, for he hears my voice. He hears my cry for mercy. Because he turns his ear to me, I will call on him as long as I live (Psalm 116).

And there is one more thing I want to share about my friend. He is a wonderful host. His dinner celebrations are a joy for the body and the soul. He prepares a table before me and makes sure that I shall lack nothing. With awe I realize that the one I love the most is now and forevermore my gracious host. I anticipate our special feasts together.

And all of you as well are invited to this same feast. The name of my friend, my personal and intimate friend, is Jesus. He also happens to be the Lord of the universe. That is why he can invite all of us so generously and sacrificially to his table. Though unseen, he meets us there in the breaking of bread.

I will kneel down at his table and acknowledge his kingship and his personal friendship in my life. His love burns in my heart like a living flame. This flame is at times so hot and so wonderfully bright that it must be shared. I consider it a duty and a privilege to witness in word and in song to the living flame of Christ's steadfast and ever-present love.

And if you think this sounds like a sentimental love letter, listen to how King David expressed himself through Psalm 116, and think of the living telephone line:

> I love the Lord for he heard my voice;
>> he heard my cry for mercy,
> Because he turned his ear to me,
>> I will call on him as long as I live. . . .
> Be at rest once more, O my soul,
>> For the Lord has been good to you.

AFTERWORD

I sit in my little house in the forest in the Ozark Mountains. It's also by the lake, so I call it Quiet Waters. I start a fire in the fireplace and watch a wonderful log burn. There was a scar where a branch had been cut off. The flames poured through it. That's like the scar in my life, I thought. When Walter left so quickly over a dozen years ago, it was like an amputation. The bleeding has stopped, the wound has healed, and I have learned to walk again, albeit with a limp. "In love's battles, only the wounded can serve," someone has said. Is that why the flame pours out so brightly where the branch has been severed?

A year ago my mother "flew away" and was united with my father after forty-eight long years of separation. Somehow I can see them sitting peaceably together holding hands and delighting in the way God blessed their obedience.

I'm thankful that I have a Friend who wants to release me from bearing needless burdens. I cannot rescue others from their struggles. Otherwise I would be like the child who tried to open a cocoon with a scissors. The butterfly died. Rather I place them confidently in the hands of my heavenly Friend, knowing that "such confidence as this is ours through Christ before God. Not that we are competent to claim anything for ourselves, but our competence comes from God" (2 Cor. 3:4, 5, NIV).

I recall that first letter I received from Walter when he told me that I should walk on the earth like Jesus did. I've tried.

Not long ago I discovered an unpretentious cardboard box filled with Walter's journals, written before we were married. He had always promised me that someday he would take time to read them to me so that I could share that part of his life. But that day never came. I picked up the one entitled "Rock Island" and found the date of January 23, 1949, the day I was commissioned for missionary service in Africa. Our pastor had invited him to attend the service. I remember vaguely seeing Walter cross my path in the parish hall that evening and wondering why he was there.

Here's what he wrote: "Cleaned my room. Went to the service at First Lutheran Church for Miss Ingrid Hult. She's 22. Clear, committed, ready for any battle, and yet every inch a woman. Such a person I would marry without a moment's hesitation."

Why did I have to wait more than forty years to read those words? Maybe they mean more now. They express what I've wished to share about the confident woman, one who is clear and has her goals and purposes straight, one who is committed, one who's ready for any battle and yet remains a woman.

NOTES

Introduction

1. Linda Leonard, *The Wounded Woman* (Boston & London, Shambhala, 1985), 35.

Chapter 1. Knowing Who You Are

1. Eleanor Roosevelt, *You Learn by Living* (New York: Harper and Brothers, 1960), 63.
2. Ingrid Trobisch, *The Joy of Being a Woman* (New York: Harper & Row, 1975).
3. Gail Sheehy, *Passages* (New York: Bantam Books, 1976), 93–94.
4. Ibid, 94.
5. Henrik Ibsen, *The Dollhouse* (New York: E. P. Dutton, 1975), 64–65.
6. Gail Sheehy, *Passages,* notes adapted from Chapter 2, "Predictable Crises of Adulthood," 29–47.
7. Robert G. and Mary C. Wells, *Menopause and Mid-life* (Wheaton, IL: Tyndale House, 1990), 29.
8. C. S. Lewis, *The Problem of Pain* (New York: Macmillan Publishing Co., 1977), 81.

Chapter 2. Learning to Accept Yourself

1. Martin Luther, *Heidelberg Dissertations: Luther's Works, vol. 31, Career of the Reformer: I* (Philadelphia: Muhlenberg Press, 1957), 57.
2. Theodor Bovet, *Die Liebe ist in unserer Mitte* (Tuebingen: Katzmann Verlag), 177.
3. *Journal of the American Dietetic Association,* October 1991.
4. Alan Loy McGinnis, *Confidence* (Minneapolis: Augsburg Publishing House, 1987), 32.
5. John and Paula Sanford, *Restoring the Christian Family* (Tulsa, OK: Victory House, 1979), 76–84.
6. Lyle Dorsett, *And God Came In* (Wheaton, IL: Crossways, 1991), 117.

7. Robert Johnson, *We: Understanding the Psychology of Romantic Love* (San Francisco: Harper & Row, 1983), 195.

8. Leanne Payne, *Restoring the Christian Soul* (Wheaton, IL: Crossways, 1991), 48–49.

9. Linda Leonard, *On the Way to the Wedding* (Boston, London: Shambhala, 1986). The concept of "feminine spirit" and "masculine heart" is found throughout the book.

10. Macrina Wiederkehr, *A Tree Full of Angels* (San Francisco: Harper & Row, 1988), 108.

11. Eleanor Roosevelt, *You Learn by Living* (New York: Harper and Brothers, 1960), 66–67.

12. Norman Wright, "When Mom Is a Perfectionist," *Focus on the Family* (Pomona, CA: August 1991), 2, 3.

Chapter 3. Discovering Your Place in This World

1. Laura Ingalls Wilder and Rose Wilder Lane, *A Little House Sampler* (New York: Harper & Row, 1988), 95.

2. Carole Streeter, *Women Alone* (Wheaton, IL: Victor Books, 1987), 68.

3. Walter Trobisch, *My Journey Homeward* (Ann Arbor, MI: Servant Publications, Vine Books, 1986), 20, 21.

Chapter 4. Using Your Gifts and Developing Skills

1. *Christianity Today,* March 4, 1988, 34.

2. H. Norman Wright, *Always Daddy's Girl* (Ventura, CA: Regal Books, 1989), 83.

3. Gail Sheehy, *Pathfinders* (New York: Bantam Books, 1981), 231. Sheehy refers to mentors here as "polestars" and "survivor guides."

4. Rollo May, *The Courage to Create* (New York: Norton, 1975), 44.

Chapter 5. Living Confidently with Other Women

1. Eunice Will, "Mother, A Memorial Tribute," *The Lutheran Ambassador* (Minneapolis, MN, April 28, 1992, vol. 30, No. 9), 6, 7.

2. Lynn Johnston, "For Better or for Worse," *The News-Leader,* Springfield, MO, 1991.

3. Anne Lindbergh, *Gift from the Sea* (New York: Vintage Books, 1978), 100.

4. Elizabeth Fishel, *Sisters* (New York: Bantom Books, 1979), 213.

5. Margaret Mead, *Blackberry Winter: My Earlier Years* (New York: William Morrow & Company, Inc., 1972), 70.

6. Sheila Kitzinger, *Giving Birth* (New York: Taplinger, 1971), 187.

Chapter 6. The Confident Single Woman

1. Streeter, *Women Alone,* 19.

2. Ibid, 18.

3. Rebecca Manley Pippert, *Hope Has Its Reasons* (San Francisco: Harper & Row, 1989), 124.

4. Walter Trobisch, *Love Is a Feeling to Be Learned* (Downers Grove, IL: InterVarsity Press, 1971), 18.

5. John Catoir and Joseph R. Thomas, *Family Matters* (New York: The Christopher Book, 1986), 99–102.

6. Streeter, *Women Alone,* 11–19.

7. Dietrich Bonhoeffer, *Letters and Papers from Prison* (London: Fontana, 1953), 163.

8. Derek Prince, *God Is a Matchmaker* (Old Tappan, NJ: Fleming H. Revell, Chosen Books, 1986), 155.

Chapter 7. Confident in Marriage

1. Marjorie Holmes, *A Time to Love* (published by C. R. Gibson in 1976). Used by permission from the author.

2. Walter Trobisch, *The Complete Works of Walter Trobisch* (Downers Grove, IL: InterVarsity Press, 1987), 580, 585. This volume is an anthology of the twelve books written by Walter Trobisch including *The Misunderstood Man,* later known as *All a Man Can Be.*

3. Robert Bly, notes taken from his interview with Bill Moyers on Public Broadcasting System, *A Gathering of Men,* 1989.

4. Alice Miller, *The Drama of the Gifted Child: The Search of the True Self* (New York: Basic Books, 1981), 15. I have used here Robert Bly's paraphrase.

5. C. S. Lewis, *Mere Christianity* (New York: Macmillan, 1952), 92.

6. John and Paula Sanford, *The Transformation of the Inner Man* (Tulsa, OK: Victory House, 1979), 270.

7. Jim and Sally Conway, *Traits of a Lasting Marriage* (Downers Grove, IL: InterVarsity Press, 1991), 37–38.

8. Pat and Jill Williams, *Rekindled* (Old Tappan, NJ: Fleming H. Revell, Chosen Books, 1991).

Chapter 8. Confident with Children

1. O. E. Rölvaag, *Giants in the Earth* (New York: Harper and Brothers, 1927), 245.

2. Susan and John Yates, *What Really Matters at Home* (Dallas: Word Publishing, 1992), 30.

3. Michael R. Phillips, *George MacDonald, Scotland's Beloved Story Teller* (Minneapolis, MN: Bethany House, 1987), 251.

4. Joseph Bayly, *Psalms of My Life* (Wheaton, IL: Tyndale House, 1969), 12. Used by permission.

5. A very helpful booklet on fertility appreciation, *The Wonder of Me: Fertility Appreciation for Adolescents and Parents* by Dr. Ruth Taylor and Ann Nerbun (published by DEPPA, P. O. Box 383, Sumter, SC 29151).

6. Richard Foster, *Prayer* (San Francisco: HarperSanFrancisco, 1992), 209–10.

Chapter 9. Hidden Strength in Suffering

1. Edith Schaeffer, *Affliction* (Old Tappan, NJ: Fleming H. Revell, Chosen Books, 1978), 212.

2. Taken from a newspaper clipping, *The News-Leader* (Springfield, MO).

3. Adapted from *Practical Christianity*, article on "Loneliness" by Ingrid Trobisch (Wheaton, IL: Tyndale House, 1987), 262–264. This book is a handbook on all aspects of Christian living with contributions from a hundred Christian writers and speakers.

4. Walter Trobisch, *Love Is a Feeling to Be Learned* (Downers Grove, IL: InterVarsity Press, 1971), 14.

5. Paula Ripple, *When Son or Daughter Divorce,* Care Notes (St. Meinrod, IN: Abbey Press, 1989).

6. Luci Shaw, personal letter, 1986.

7. Anne Lindbergh, *Hour of Gold, Hour of Lead* (New York: Harcourt Brace Jovanovich, 1973), 215.

8. Judith Fabisch, Taken from Ingrid Trobisch, *Learning to Walk Alone* (Ann Arbor, MI: Servant Books, 1985), 81.

9. Joshua Loth Liebman, *Peace of Mind* (Taken from Granger Westberg, *Good Grief,* Philadelphia: Fortress Press, 1962), 60

10. "Peanuts," *San Francisco Chronicle,* Oct. 4, 1983 (Cartoon).

11. John B. Pearrell, "Where Is God When I'm Hurting?" (*Practical Christianity,* see Note 3), 320–22.

12. Richard Foster, *Prayer* (San Francisco: HarperSanFrancisco, 1992), 220–21

Chapter 10. Goals and Guidance

1. Walter Trobisch, *My Journey Homeward* (Ann Arbor, MI: Servant Books, 1986), 24–27.

2. Madame Jeanne Guyon, *Experiencing the Depths of Jesus Christ* (Augusta, ME: Christian Books, 1981), 114.

3. Ibid, 115.

4. Ibid, 134.

Chapter 11. Use of Time

1. Anne Lindbergh, *Gift from the Sea* (New York: Vintage Books, 1978), 117.

2. Julia von Bodelschwingh, Translated from German by Ingrid Trobisch.

3. Jean Chittister, *Wisdom Distilled From the Daily* (San Fransisco: HarperSanFrancisco, 1991), 97.

4. Ibid, 101.

Chapter 12. Friendship with God

1. Renovaré, P. O. Box 879, Witchita, KS 67210-0879.

2. Eugene Peterson, *Run with the Horses* (Downers Grove, IL: InterVarsity Press, 1983), 89.

3. Maxine Glaz, "Living Beyond the Babble" (Chicago, IL: *The Lutheran,* May 1, 1991), 10.

4. Dallas Willard, *The Spirit of the Disciplines* (San Francisco: Harper & Row, 1988), 165.

5. Jean-Pierre de Caussade, *The Sacrament of the Present Moment* (San Francisco: Harper & Row, 1982), Introduction XIV.